VICTORIAN WORK

By the same author:

The History of Redditch and the Locality.

VICTORIAN WORKHOUSE

A Study of the Bromsgrove Union Workhouse 1836-1901

by

Neville Land, B.A., D.P.S.E. (Hist).,
F.R.S.A., F.Coll.P., F.R.G.S.

BREWIN BOOKS

First published by Brewin Books of Studley
in December 1990

ISBN 0 947731 69 5

THIS
PAPER
CONTAINS
STRAW
PULP
TO HELP OUR ENVIRONMENT

Typeset in Baskerville 11pt.
Made and printed in Great Britain by
Supaprint (Redditch)Ltd.

ACKNOWLEDGEMENTS

This book is dedicated to my mother

Mr. A.M. Wherry, B.A., D.A.A. County Archivist.
The staff of the "Hereford and Worcester Record Office".
County Hall, Worcester.
Mr. D.J. Drewitt, B.A., A.L.A., Bromsgrove Library.
Mr. P.J. Davis, B.A., A.L.A., Redditch Library.
Mr. W.J. Kings, Bromsgrove Society.
Dr. Allan Richards, Bromsgrove Society.
Mrs. J.E. Mayne, B.A.
Forge Mill Museum, Redditch.
Mrs. Cheryl A. Tedstone.
Mrs. Doreen Clarke, Bridley Moor High School.
Mrs. Christine A. Haynes, Bridley Moor High School.
Mr. M. Marshall, General Manager of the Bromsgrove General
    Hospital.
Mrs. Pauline Jones, Clerical Dept. of the Bromsgrove General
    Hospital.
Mr. P. Amphlett.
Mrs. A. Pettigrew.
"The Bromsgrove Messenger".
"The Worcester Journal".
County Museum, Hartlebury.
Mrs. M. Twist, Birmingham City Centre Library.

ILLUSTRATIONS

CONTENTS

Page

INTRODUCTION

The unmarked graves in a long forgotten corner of the public cemetery in my home town, first drew my attention to the unfortunate paupers of the nineteenth century. The crime of many was simply to be luckless enough to lose employment, for which they were categorised as the "able-bodied poor", and they and their families were then put in the first institution of modern history - the workhouse.

The New Poor Law and the workhouse system lasted from 1834 until 1929 before the abolition of the Boards of Guardians. Responsibility for the workhouse then fell to the County Councils until 1948 when the National Insurance Act and the dawn of the Welfare State put a final end to the institution. Many of the workhouses then became part of the new hospitals of the post war period.

Today's affluent society is protected from "the cradle to the grave" by a multitude of welfare measures; benefits most of us take for granted.

The book, most of which is based on the minute books of the Bromsgrove Workhouse Union 1836 to 1901, focuses on these less enlightened times.

CHAPTER ONE

NATIONAL ATTITUDES TOWARDS PAUPERISM
1600 - 1834

1. The Old Poor Law of 1601
2. Speenhamland System of 1795
3. The Poor Law Amendment Act of 1834

The poor were often sustained by the large number of monasteries in England and Wales until their dissolution in the sixteenth century in the reign of Henry VIII. After the 1540's however, the problem of pauperism increased, made worse by the disbanding of private armies and especially by the spread of Tudor enclosures. Many paupers were forced to become beggars and some banded or grouped together to terrorise small villages. These two lines from a contemporary poem refer to the increasing problem:-

"Hark, hark the dogs do bark
The beggars are coming to town".

The government adopted a very hard stance against the beggars, and in 1598 and 1601 the 'Old Poor Law' was founded in the reign of Elizabeth I. 'The Acte for the Releife of the Poore' passed in 1598 formed the basis of the reform. It established a system of relief for the poor based on the collection of a poll tax called the poor rate. Each parish had to pay the tax and the J.P's of the day monitored its progress. In the reign of Charles II, the Act of Settlement of 1662 strengthened the system. The poor were put into three categories. The impotent or helpless poor or non-able bodied poor including the old, sick, crippled and children were given constructive help. Outdoor relief in the form of bread was often delivered to their homes, and children of the poor were apprenticed at the expense of the parish. The second category was the able-bodied poor, who through no fault of their own, were unable to find work. This group was accommodated in workhouses, and the overseers brought in "a stock of flax, hemp, wool, thread, iron and other stuff to set the poor to work". The goods produced were sold,

SCHEDULE A.

Containing the Forms of the Parish Accounts to be kept by the Churchwardens and Overseers of the Parish of

FORM 1.—*The Rate Book.*

No. of Assessment.	Name of Occupier.	Number of Votes.	Name of Owner.	Number of Votes.	Description of Property, whether Land or Houses, &c., and Situation or Name of Property.	If Land, the presumed Number of Acres.	Rental or Annual Value of Property.	Amount at which the Property is assessed.	Amount of Poor Rate to be collected at in the Pound.	Amount of Arrear of former Rate, if any.	Total Amount to be collected.	Amount actually collected.	Present Arrear.	Amount not recoverable, or legally excused.

*Note.—*In estimating the number of Votes to which an Owner is entitled, the Assessments of the several Properties in respect of which he is entitled to vote must be added together, and the number of his Votes must be inserted in the place in which his name occurs in the Rate Book.

The Rate Book. The relief for the poor was obtained from the poor rate collected from within the Union. The money was spent on outdoor (at home) relief or indoor relief (workhouse relief mainly for the able-bodied and families)

2

and the profits were used to supplement the poor relief collection from the parish. As soon as the job prospects improved in the parish the able-bodied were encouraged to leave the work-house. The third group were the rogues and vagabonds who were virtually professional beggars. This group was treated harshly in an attempt to stamp out the sturdy beggar element in the society. Begging was made illegal, and punished by flogging, or by a prison sentence in a house of correction, or even hanging. The Act of 1662 decreed that all poor persons had to be looked after in the parish of their birth, and this law led to some drastic measures over the centuries, such as the forceful return of pregnant but unmarried women back to their home parishes.

In the eighteenth century the Elizabethan and Stuart poor laws were added to. The Act of 1722 allowed, but did not compel groups of neighbouring parishes to form themselves into Unions and to build one workhouse for the Union or collection of parishes. Those applying for help could then be sent to the Union workhouse where the bare needs of food and shelter were provided. It was hoped that the workhouse would only attract the desperate poor to apply for such indoor relief. This belief was called the "workhouse test". By the late 1770's unemployment was on the increase especially in agricultural areas where the enclosure movement was causing social hardships, and a drift of the landless labourers towards the industrial towns was the inevitable result. Workhouses soon found themselves full as the social problems escalated. A new Act, known as 'Gilbert's Act' was therefore passed in 1782 and this gave greater encouragement to the setting up of Unions of parishes with common workhouses. It also stressed that when an able-bodied man applied for poor relief, work must be found for him near his own home and that he should not be sent to the workhouse. Often the parish, however, was unable to find work for him and he was then paid for doing worthless work. The J.P's also found themselves at a loss of how to tackle the problem.

The last few years of the eighteenth century saw problems of poverty greatly escalate due to various factors such as rising unemployment, increasing bread costs, economic dislocation caused by the French Wars, the worsening inflation and fall in real wages. Various schemes were adopted by parishes to combat the escalating problem of pauperism. In much of the north of England, the parishes regularly paid outdoor relief to poor families if the family was only temporarily out of work, due, for instance, to a short period of recession and unemployment. Another scheme was the Labour Rate, whereby ratepayers could choose either to pay their rates or to employ a certain number of paupers for a given length of service. The employers, such as farmers could choose his labourers and there was often competition for the best workers. Another scheme was the Roundsman system where the able-bodied pauper labourers were employed in turn or in 'rounds' by the farmer poor relief payers in a parish, and if the farmer paid insufficient wages, then the wages were topped up from parish poor relief. The most widely adopted scheme, however, was the 'Speenhamland System'; so named, when in May 1795 twenty Berkshire magistrates met at the 'Pelican Inn' in Speen near Newbury to discuss the problem of pauperism. Speenhamland never became a parliamentary Act, but it came into widespread use in the Southern and central parts of England.

The original Speenhamland Scheme was based on an agreed poverty line. This poverty line was adjusted according to the cost of bread and the size of the pauper family. Families who were below the poverty line were given allowances in bread, flour or money to bring them up to the mark. It was a constructive attempt to bring some order into the chaos of the structure of the 15,000 separate parishes of England and Wales. Part of the Speenhamland order read as follows . . . . "The magistrates make the following calculations and allowance for the relief of all industrious men and their families who shall endeavour for their own support and maintenance."

"That is to say, when the gallon loaf shall cost 1 shilling (5p) then every poor and industrious man shall have for his own support 3 shillings (15p) weekly, either produced by his own or his family's labour, or an allowance from the poor rates; and for the support of his wife and every other of his family, 1s 6d (7½p). And as the price of bread rises or falls 3d to the man and 1d to every other of the family and every 1d which the loaf rise above 1 shilling". The average labourers wage at the beginning of the nineteenth century was approximately 7 shillings (35p) a week.

According to some historians, Speenhamland was introduced at a crucial political time in our history, and that its beneficial impacts saved England from a national famine and a national revolution. Others became hostile to Speenhamland as the associated poor relief costs escalated. This anti-Speenhamland lobby influenced by Jeremy Bentham regarded the drain of national resources on the minority as a sinful excessive waste. Many also embraced the beliefs of the Rev. Thomas Malthus who suggested that the increased pauper population would stretch the national resources to

4

breaking point. His publication of 1798 "An Essay on the Principle of Population" argued that population tended to increase at a faster rate than its food supplies, unless it was checked by poverty, epidemics, famines and smaller families. This lobby identified Speenhamland and its allowance system as a major reason for larger families. The fear of a population explosion was a deep seated one and even prompted the government to accept John Rickman's idea for a national census in 1801. Malthus' unsympathetic attitude to poverty as illustrated below was adopted by many and encouraged by well known economists such as David Ricardo.

"The labouring poor always live hand to mouth. Their wants of the moment are all they think about and they seldom think of the future. All they have above their needs of the moment goes, generally speaking, to the ale house".

A cartoon depicting a workhouse yard illustrating the splitting up of families.

Clamour for the reform of the Old Poor Law and especially the Speenhamland content gathered from the mid 1820's. Official statistics revealed that money spent on the poor rose from £2 million in 1784 to approximately £7 million in 1832. Population increases in the period from approximately 3½ million to approximately 7 million seemed to clarify and intensify Malthusian warnings. However, blame cannot be placed entirely on Speenhamland for these figures. Research has revealed that in Sussex, "the most notorious Speenhamland county" agricultural wages were higher than in any county in the South except those nearest to the capital. Furthermore, population increases in so called Speenhamland counties after 1821 were below the national average for rural areas. Some recent research even suggests that some Speenhamland counties were experiencing a decline in population due to increasing migration.

However, in 1832 the Whig government decided on a thorough examination of the Old Poor Law, and set up a Royal Commission. This body undertook the most detailed social investigation ever undertaken in Britain up to that time. Twenty-six investigators visited about 3,000 townships and parishes throughout England and Wales in the late months of 1832. Two points must be borne in mind however. Firstly it is claimed by some critics of the Commission, amongst them the famous Webbs, authors of the well known 'English Poor Law History' that many of the investigators were influenced by Benthamite and Malthusian thinking, and that they therefore had a blinkered and pre-conceived idea of what its findings should reveal. Secondly, the set questionnaires of the Commission were only answered by approximately 10% of the 15,000 parishes of England and Wales, and that the Commission produced some misleading facts and conclusions from these returns.

Speenhamland was severely attacked by the Royal Commission. It was accused of encouraging idleness, of taking away the pride of the independent labourer, of discouraging paupers from saving, of encouraging labourers to marry at an early age and have large families. The Commission also associated Speenhamland with corruption of minor officials such as the overseers, and for encouraging the permissive society which resulted in increasing illegitimacy and drunkenness. The Commission was scathing of the high costs associated with the Old Poor Law, and quoted evidence from Cholesbury, a village that had been made bankrupt because of high poor rates. The recommendations of the Royal Commission included the restoration of the pride of the independent labourer by a dramatic reduction in the allowance system. It suggested that relief should only be given to those in real need, and that 'the workhouse test' should be vigorously re-inforced.

Assistant Commissioner, Edwin Chadwick and Commissioner Nassau Senior wrote most of the Commission's report which came out in February 1834. These two central figures were influenced by Malthus; and Chadwick was a keen disciple of Benthamite thinking. The Report became a best seller. Ten thousand copies were given away to stimulate public opinion and a further ten thousand were sold. The Whig government accepted the Report and it formed the basis for the 'Poor Law Amendment Act' which became law later on in the year. This new legislation effectively ended the Old Poor Law which had been in use, in one form or another, since Elizabethan times. Many mourned its passing. Dr. Blang's recent comments included the following "The Old Poor Law was a welfare state in miniature", a reference to its attempts at family allowances and unemployment compensation schemes. The Old Poor Law was flexible and sensitive to human needs and also adaptable over the years. J.D. Marshall in a recent publication condemned the Poor Law Commission of 1832 with these words, that it - - - - - - - "lacked the data to look forward with hope, and therefore humanity and - - - - - - - looked backward and condemned".

Strong views have been expressed on the "New Poor Law Amendment Act of 1834" especially its workhouse system. Charles Dickens' feelings were made clear in his novel 'Oliver Twist' which featured the life of an orphan boy, who was born and reared in the workhouse. "The bowls never wanted washing. The boys polished them with their spoons till they shone again." The novelist's biting sarcasm is displayed in the following few lines in his description of the Board of Guardians . . . "the members of the Board were very wise men. . . . so they established the rule that all poor should have the alternative of being starved by a gradual process in the workhouse, or by a quick one out of it. . . . . They made a great many other wise and humane regulations; kindly undertook to divorce poor married persons (a reference to the rule of separating the family on its arrival in the workhouse) . . . and instead of compelling a man to support his family, took his family away from him and made him a bachelor".

Politician Benjamin Disraeli said of the 1834 Act that it "announced to the world, that in England, poverty is a crime".

Writer Thomas Carlyle echoed the feelings of Richard Oastler and John Fielden when he remarked "The New Poor

Law is an announcement . . . . that whosoever will not work
ought not to live.   Can the poor man that is willing to work
always find work, and live by his work?   A man willing but
unable to find work is the saddest under the sun".   The Rev.
Joseph Stephens, a contemporary of the above echoed the
feelings of most of the industrial north of England's opposition   "The people are not going to stand this.   I will say
that sooner than wife and husband and father and son shall
be sundered and dungeoned and fed on skillee - sooner than
wife and daughter shall wear the prison dress, sooner than
that - Newcastle ought to be, and shall be one blaze of fire
with only one way to put it out, and that with the blood of
all who support this abominable measure".   The workers of
the north opposed the new Act because of its inflexibility.
In Nottingham in 1836-7 the Board of Guardians tried their
best to accommodate 700 persons in a workhouse only
meant for 520 persons, rather than grant outdoor relief to
many of their number.

ANNO QUARTO & QUINTO

GULIELMI IV. REGIS.

★ ★ ★ ★ ★ ★ ★ ● ● ★

C A P. LXXVI.

An Act for the Amendment and better Administration of the Laws relating to the Poor in
England and *Wales.*   [14th *August* 1834.]

WHEREAS it is expedient to alter and amend the Laws
relating to the Relief of poor Persons in *England* and
Wales : Be it therefore enacted by the King's most
Excellent Majesty, by and with the Advice and Consent of the Lords
Spiritual and Temporal, and Commons, in this present Parliament
assembled, and by the Authority of the same, That it shall be lawful **Appointment**
for His Majesty, His Heirs and Successors, by Warrant under the **and Removal**
Royal Sign Manual, to appoint Three fit Persons to be Commissioners **of Commis-**
to carry this Act into execution, and also from Time to Time, at **sioners.**
pleasure, to remove any of the Commissioners for the Time being,
and upon every or any Vacancy in the said Number of Commissioners,
either by Removal or by Death or otherwise, to appoint some other
fit Person to the said Office ; and until such Appointment it shall be
lawful for the surviving or continuing Commissioners or Commissioner
to act as if no such Vacancy had occurred.

8

II. And be it further enacted, That the said Commissioners shall be styled " The Poor Law Commissioners for *England* and *Wales* ;" and the said Commissioners, or any Two of them, may sit, from Time to Time as they deem expedient, as a Board of Commissioners for car- rying this Act into execution ; and the said Commissioners acting as such Board shall be and are hereby empowered, by Summons under their Hands and Seal, to require the Attendance of all such Persons as they may think fit to call before them upon any Question or Matter
connected

XXIII. And be it further enacted, That it shall be lawful for the said Commissioners, and they are hereby empowered, from Time to Time when they may see fit, by any Writing under their Hands and Seal, by and with the Consent in Writing of a Majority of the Guardians of any Union, or with the Consent of a Majority of the Rate-payers and Owners of Property entitled to vote in manner herein-after pre- scribed, in any Parish, such last-mentioned Majority to be ascertained in manner provided in and by this Act, to order and direct the Over- seers or Guardians of any Parish or Union not having a Workhouse or Workhouses to build a Workhouse or Workhouses, and to purchase or hire Land for the Purpose of building the same thereon, or to purchase or hire a Workhouse or Workhouses, or any Building or Buildings for the Purpose of being used as or converted into a Workhouse or Work- houses ; and, with the like Consent, to order and direct the Overseers or Guardians of any Parish or Union having a Workhouse or Work- houses, or any Buildings capable of being converted into a Workhouse or Workhouses, to enlarge or alter the same in such Manner as the said Commissioners shall deem most proper for carrying the Provisions of this Act into execution, or to build, hire, or purchase any addi- tional Workhouse or Workhouses, or any Building or Buildings for the Purpose of being used as or converted into a Workhouse or Work- houses, or to purchase or hire any Land for building such additional Workhouse or Workhouses thereon, of such Size and Description, and according to such Plan, and in such Manner as the said Commissioners shall deem most proper for carrying the Provisions of this Act into execution ; and the Overseers and Guardians to whom any such Order shall be directed are hereby authorized and required to assess, raise, and levy such Sum or Sums of Money as may be necessary for the Purposes specified in such Order, by such Powers, Ways, and Means as are now by Law given to or vested in Churchwardens and Overseers or Guardians of the Poor for purchasing or hiring Land, or for building, hiring, and maintaining Workhouses for the Use of the Poor, in their respective Parishes or Unions, or to borrow Money for such Purposes under the Provisions of this or any other Act or Acts.

XXIV. And be it further enacted, That for the better and more effec- tually securing the Repayment of any Sum or Sums of Money which may be borrowed for the Purposes aforesaid, with Interest, it shall be lawful for the said Overseers or Guardians to charge the future Poor Rates of such Parish or Union with the Amount of such Sum or Sums of Money : Provided always, that the Principal Sum or Sums to be raised for such Purposes, whether raised within the Year or borrowed, shall in no Case exceed the average annual Amount of
the

The introduction of the "Poor Law Amendment Act"
of 1834

Workhouses were despised to such an extent in certain areas that they became commonly known as 'bastilles', a reference to the dreaded prison fortress in Paris which was destroyed by the revolutionaries of July 1789. In Bradford, Yorkshire in 1837 there was intense public agitation against the New Poor Law Amendment Act. The Board of Guardians was set upon by the crowd and driven from their venue, the local courthouse. They sheltered in a nearby hotel, where they were besieged by a hostile mob. Eventually special constables and even a cavalry force were called before order was restored.

The following ballad was published in Bradford in the late 1830's and illustrates the depth of feeling in the industrial north.

"Come yon men and women unto me attend,
And listen and see what for you I have penned;
And if you do buy it, and carefully read,
'T will make your hearts within you to bleed.

The lions at London, with their cruel paw,
You know they have passed a Starvation Law,
These tigers and wolves should be chained in a den,
Without power to worry poor women and men.

When a man and his wife for sixty long years
Have toiled together, through troubles and fears
And brought up a family with prudence and care
To be sent to the Bastille it's very unfair.

And in the Bastille each woman and man
Is parted asunder - is this a good plan?
A word of sweet comfort they cannot express
For unto each other they ne'er have access.

You give them hard labour, it is understood
In handmills the grain they must grind for their bread,
Like men in a prison they work them in gangs,
With turning and twisting it fills them with pangs".

There were riots against the N.P.L.A.A. in other parts as well as in Bradford. Dewsbury and Todmorden experienced them in 1838. After these experiences the Poor Law Commissioners had to tread very carefully in the militant areas of the West Riding of Yorkshire and Lancashire. Most Unions regarded all paupers between the ages of 16 and 70 as being 'able-bodied'. If the head of the family received relief, then the whole family was registered as paupers, and sent to the workhouse.

A cartoon published in 1836

A cartoon published in 1836 depicting the changing attitude of the government towards pauperism before and after the introduction of the 1834 Act.

Deep feelings about the workhouse persisted. Even in 1892 George Lansbury gave a vivid and black account based on a visit to a London workhouse.

Actor Charles Chaplin in his autobiography had a deep and personal experience of the workhouse in the 1890's. . . . . "Then the forlorn bewilderment of it struck me: for there we were made to separate, Mother going in one direction to the women's ward, and me in another to the children's . . . . The shock of seeing Mother enter the visiting room garbed in workhouse clothes. How forlorn and embarrassed she looked! In one week she had aged and grown thin".

The propaganda against the workhouse system of 1834 was given an immense boost by a very dramatic incident at Andover workhouse in 1845. The ripples from this incident, more than any other, continued and fostered the bad image of the workhouse system. The incident was sparked when certain inmates who had been set a task of breaking animal bones in the yard, resorted to eating some of the marrow and gristle from some of the bones. The press did the rest! The

11

scandal hit the Poor Law Commissioners hard. A Parliamentary Select Committee was set up in 1846 to look into the facts, and the facts were proven! Suffice to say such events were not commonplace but such a scandal did the workhouse system untold damage.

This biting poem was published in 'Punch' in 1848:-

"I'm Stephen Witcher, labouring man - of Andover I be,
A pauper of the workhouse, and a cripple in the knee,
The Guardians there have sent me out, in the cold and rain,
To sit all day, a breakin' stones in agony and pain".

"Lame as I was, I couldn't work; so what was I to do?
Unto the Board of Guardians I at last was forced to go
'Oh! Witcher,' says the Chairman - he's a parson, I should say
'We'll relieve you for a fortnight, but no longer - not one day'.

"To the workhouse on my crutches then I hobbled back again,
And begged and prayed for mercy, but my words were all in vain,
So here be I a cracking stones in misery and grief,
And this here treatment is what they calls their 'System of Relief'.

The preceding descriptions of the 1834 New Poor Law vividly illustrate the depths of feeling the system generated in the nineteenth century. Furthermore the descriptions come not only from working class people but also from well known middle class writers and thinkers, politicians and even a future Prime Minister. In defence of the 1834 System however the reader must be made aware of a few facts. Some of its aims seemed just; namely to restore the self-respect of the independent labourers; to save money for the country, and to test whether certain claimants really needed relief. Chadwick who wrote the report of 1832 was not in favour of the general type of workhouse, which sadly became the norm after 1834. He was in favour of specialization of pauper group treatment, especially the pauper ill, pauper children, and the elderly paupers, and his ideas were broadly akin to some of the ideas within our welfare state of today. Sadly, however, the quest of saving money for the nation became the overriding objective of the New Poor Law, and even Chadwick's suggestions were ignored.

The administration and organisation of the NPLAA seemed sound enough. There was an attempt at standardization of relief in well organised workhouses. Ratepayers elected a Board of Guardians to serve the Union and to regulate both indoor and outdoor relief. Many of these Guardians were well respected members of the community. Furthermore the system was a national one, replacing, it was claimed a number of archaic and wasteful schemes and services. Advocates of the new system of relief claimed that it introduced a professional structure involving salaried persons, and this alone they said would improve efficiency and stop corruption. They also claimed that a new puritan attitude came in with the 1834 Act, encouraging thrift and hard work, and that this in itself was instrumental in checking the spread of the permissive society in the nineteenth century. In addition, the NPLAA was a prototype - the first national administrative machine of modern times. the forerunner of such bodies as the Local Government Board, the Board of Education and the Ministry of Health. Advocates have also denied the change of inflexibility, and quoted examples from Unions that kept a balance between indoor and outdoor relief. Many of the newly created medical officers who were employed by the Unions were hard working and deeply conscientious men who played important roles in the reforms of public health and sanitation within the community. Defenders of the 1834 Act claim that the NPLAA was not rigid but allowed itself to be moulded and changed over the years, though as a counter-argument it must be said that many of these changes came as a result of well founded opposition and that the changes were long overdue. From the 1870's after long agitation an increasing number of workhouse children were sent to local elementary schools. The treatment of the pauper ill improved after 1865 when the 'Lancet' reported on the shocking state of the sick poor in London workhouses. The treatment of the mentally ill paupers also slowly improved after the Metropolitan Poor Act of 1867 which established separate asylums in London. Other large Unions followed the example of the Capital in succeeding years.

CHAPTER TWO

THE OFFICERS OF THE BROMSGROVE UNION

1. The beginnings of the workhouse 1836.
2. Masters and Matrons and their working relationships with fellow officers.
3. The Mr. and Mrs. Pope crisis of 1863.
4. The dismissal of Mr. Allinson, master, in 1877.
5. Death of Mr. Wyatt, master, of typhoid fever in 1889.
6. Duties of Medical Officer of Health and Medical Officer of the workhouse.
7. The fight against epidemics.
8. Dr. Kidd's disagreement with the Guardians 1891.
9. The Collector of poor rates.
10. The contrasting stories of two Relieving Officers.
11. The Chaplain of the workhouse.
12. The Clerk of the workhouse.
13. The Board of Guardians.

The inaugural meeting of the Bromsgrove Union took place on Tuesday, November 8th. 1836 in the town hall. The eight persons present included six J.P's of the locality, an M.P., and an assistant Poor Law Commissioner. The latter was Robert Neale, a representative of the government's Poor Law Commission in London, and his role was to establish guidelines for those present. Thomas Henry Cookes M.P. was accompanied by the president of the meeting, the Right Honourable and Reverend Lord Aston, and the other five gentle-men included George Francis Iddins, Thomas Moore Bartleet, Charles Noel, Frederick Smith and Thomas Prangster all gentry of well repute in the district.

The Bromsgrove Union was initially to comprise of twelve parishes and was served by eighteen guardians. These guardians were elected from the districts ratepayers and were mainly middle class in outlook. Bromsgrove was served by

14

five guardians. Tardebigge, which included the small but expanding township of Redditch was served by three guardians, and each of the other ten parishes comprising of Stoke Prior, Belbroughton, Alvechurch, Cofton Hackett, Frankley, Hagley, Pedmore, Tutnall and Cobley, Hunnington and Romsley was served by one guardian. The twelve parishes were subdivided into two districts for ease of administration.

The first official meeting of the Board of Guardians took place on Monday 21st November 1836, and this was in the old poor law workhouse in the Strand. The building was to continue as a workhouse until the new workhouse built to the New Poor Law regulations was completed at Gravel Pit Piece, one mile from the town centre in Birmingham Road. The guardians were brisk and businesslike in their manner and agreed to meet each Monday at 11.00 a.m. promptly, and this enthusiasm for their duty hardly waned over the years. A number of bye-laws were established that illustrate this early zeal "That every guardian when he has a desire to speak, shall stand up and address the Chairman, George Francis Iddins Esq., and at all other times observe strict silence, and attend the matter under discussion . . . . and if two or more guardians shall rise to speak at the same time, the Chairman shall decide to whom belongs the priority of speaking". It was decided to relieve those entitled to outdoor relief on a weekly basis, and the able bodied poor should be accommodated in the existing workhouse. It was agreed to inspect the four workhouses which had been established by the Old Poor Law in the locality; at Bromsgrove, Belbroughton, Tardebigge and Alvechurch before a decision could be made as to their future. The new workhouse would largely replace all the four old buildings, and be large enough to hold at least three hundred paupers. As well as the able bodied poor over the age of 15 years, other groups that could be housed at the new workhouse would include men and women infirm through age or any other cause, girls and boys between the ages of seven and fifteen, and also children under the age of seven. Many of these young people were to include orphans or illegitimates who stayed at the workhouse until they were old enough to be apprenticed. Old and infirm were to be brought into the workhouse if they had no families to care for them when they were incapacitated. Bromsgrove like many of the new workhouses set up by the Act of 1834 was a general workhouse and therefore accepted broad categories of paupers including lunatics and idiots. The worst cases of the mentally ill were soon to be moved to the County asylum at Powick.

The workhouse or the 'bastille' as it was called by the outraged working class was totally detested and was to be avoided at all costs until starvation would drive the poor to its door. On arrival at the workhouse, paupers suffered a further indignity; families were split and its members were separated into different parts of the workhouse, and this process was the ultimate punishment, but the Act of 1834 was adamant "This separation must be entire and absolute between the sexes, who are to live, sleep and take their meals in totally distinct and separate parts of the building with an enclosed yard for each". It is unclear how much separation was actually possible within the confines of the old workhouse in the Strand, but the new workhouse was planned according to these demands of the Act.

The first meeting also drew up a list of posts and salaries to be paid within the workhouse. The full time clerk was to keep the minute books in good order and to liaise with both guardians and employees of the Union's workhouse, and his salary was advertised at £120 p.a. The posts of the two relieving officers were advertised at £90 p.a. for the district of Bromsgrove, and £80 p.a. for the Belbroughton district.

The posts for the governor or master of the workhouse at £40 p.a. and matron at £20 p.a. were also advertised in the local press. All twelve parishes had to contribute towards the cost of poor relief within the union, but each parish paid for its own paupers and some of the small but poverty-laden parishes were soon to find themselves in financial difficulty especially at bad times of the year, namely the months of January to March when outdoor relief was at its highest. The first quarterly instalments payable to the Union from the parishes became due before the 24th December 1836 and amounted to £1,583. Bromsgrove with the highest number of paupers to support had to pay the highest relief and this came to £464. 15s. 0d. Second was Tardebigge with a sum of £279. 5s. 0d., and third was Belbroughton with a sum of £192. Romsley's contribution was the smallest amounting to £10. 5s. 0d. Until 1865 each parish remained responsible for the cost of relieving its own paupers, but the Union Chargeability Act of 1865 was an attempt to spread the cost amongst all parishes within the Union. The payment of poor relief was resented by all those who had to pay, and was the forerunner of the rates payments within our modern communities.

The Act of 1834 also placed an emphasis on the Union's responsibilities towards the health and sanitation of the parishes, and for this purpose it was divided into four medical districts; Bromsgrove, Tardebigge, Alvechurch and Belbroughton, each with its own Medical Officer, on an average salary of fifty pounds each per annum.

The front of the Bromsgrove Union Workhouse 1838-1948

By the sixteenth meeting of the Board of Guardians in early March 1837 a number of targets had been achieved. An official order was placed for the three acre site of the new workhouse. Tenders for a variety of provisions for the workhouse were released, scrutinized and accepted and included products such as bread, flour, beef, mutton, bacon, cheese, potatoes, oatmeal, peas, rice, butter, starch, pepper, treacle, soap, candles and rushlights, tea, sugar, vinegar, coals, hats, strong dark coloured cloth, coats, waistcoats, trousers, shoes and flannel. Almost invariably the lowest quotes were accepted. A Mr. Joseph Greening was appointed to serve the Union with some of its produce at the following prices. East India rice at 21/- per cwt, black tea at 3/6d per cwt, starch at 6/- per lb, treacle at 3½d per lb, candles and rush at 6/- per dozen, vinegar at 1/6d per gallon. Other accepted tenders included a supply of cheese at 41/- per cwt and peas at 7s 6d per bushell. Even bulk tenders for coffins were scrutinized before the price was agreed. "Moved by John Merry, Esq., and seconded by Mr. Cordell that Mr. John Tipper have the contract for coffins, large and small, ledged lid, to be oiled, and properly pitched, with two letters on the lid and cord handles at 5/9 each delivered to the workhouse, and at 7s 3d each delivered at any other place within the union". On death the pauper was placed in his cheap coffin with no lining and no shroud, and was taken on his final journey in a handcart pulled by old men. The pauper was laid to rest in an unmarked grave in the section of the public cemetery reserved for the workhouse.

A number of appointments had been filled by February 1837 including those for relieving officers, medical officers, and workhouse master and matron. The latter posts, were filled by a Mr. William Owen and his wife Lucy. By March 1837 a registrar of 'Births and Deaths' was appointed in the Union in keeping with the demand of new national legislation. Within the first year the Board's stance towards paupers and employees was established. In mid January 1837 concern was expressed over the deaths of three outdoor relieved paupers. "It appearing from the relieving officer's application book for the Bromsgrove districts, that a pauper of Tardebigge has died leaving no means to defray the expense of his burial - ordered that the cost of his burial be paid to the pauper in the out relief book". The Board had little mercy on employees who failed in their duties. Dr. Kendwick, Medical Officer of the Bromsgrove district being censured in February 1837 for falsifying a return on a patient, claiming a fee for visiting a dying man. The same doctor was forced to resign in May 1837 for committing a similar offence. The Board of Guardians attitude to the expense of maintaining illegitimate children illustrates the prevailing mood of this Victorian period, for in May 1837 they ordered a list of all bastards receiving parochial relief, and by June the list had been drawn up and the parents targetted. The shame list contained 48 illegitimate children between the ages of one year and nine years, and also the names of the parents and orders placed upon the parents to meet expenses. It contained the following three sections e.g.

	ENTRY 1	ENTRY 2	ENTRY 3
Mother's name	Harriett Carter	Maria Peat	Ann Vincent
Father's name	Samuel Tongue	William Pitts	Thomas Horton
Father's address	Bentley	Redditch	Redditch
Order on Father	1s/6d	2s/6d	2/-
Order on Mother	1/-	6d	6d
Arrears	£2. 10s. 0d.	£2. 0s. 0d.	£2. 0s. 0d.
Comments	Father is village blacksmith	The father transported	Father gone to America.

The Union had to begrudgingly accept the fact that Botany Bay, Australia and America were beyond their reach.

18

The building of the new workhouse made good progress in the first year. Six tenders were received for building the workhouse ranging from £6,200 to £5,150, and in keeping with custom the guardians adopted the lowest tender by a Mr. Edward Clarke of Leamington. An additional £440 was paid for the three acre plot. By September the contractor had made reasonable progress and was paid the first installments amounting to £450. The board, however, was to regret its decision to accept this tender as the Leamington contractor became bankrupt in April 1838. Another builder was employed to finish the workhouse, and it was eventually opened in the Spring of 1839.

The Guardians were an industrious lot and accepted without question all the instructions received from the Poor Law Commission in London. They even convened a meeting on Boxing Day 1836. Their early obedience to the Act is seen in the body of their first six month report to Commissioners in May 1837 "That your petitioners having for the last six months been actively engaged in carrying the provisions of the New Poor Law Amendment Act into effect, feel great satisfaction in stating their convictions, that the present system of administering relief to the poor is calculated to benefit all classes of community and has fully answered their most sanguine expectations. . . . . The New Poor Law will prove highly conducive to the public welfare by affording more effective relief to the really necessitous and removing those inducements to idleness and pauperism which notoriously existed under the Old System, at the same time giving every encouragement to the independent labourers".

The Board of Guardians was responsible for the appointments and dismissals of all staff working within the Bromsgrove Union. The Guardians advertised posts in the local and regional press and always asked for CV's. Their appointments were not always wise, and there was a frequent turnover of staff. The Guardians rarely unanimously agreed on an appointment and the compromise candidate was sometimes lacking in qualities. Such a mistake was made in 1862 when Mr. and Mrs. Pope were appointed as the new master and matron, and I have included details of this in the chapter entitled 'Crises'. Lax behaviour amongst the staff was not condoned and often meant an instant dismissal. Rates of pay were the average, and the Board sometimes kept wages low until the recipient was forced to ask for more remuneration. Sometimes the Board begrudgingly raised the salary, and at other times they ignored the plea, and on some rare occasions even asked the employee to leave office. The relationship therefore between the Board and the officials was extremely formal and businesslike.

The most important officer was the master of the workhouse. He had the most difficult of all tasks, and had to liaise with his staff and the rigid Board of Guardians. A tremendous amount of responsibility was placed on him on the day to day running of the house including controlling the paupers, and staff, ordering provisions and balancing the books. He had to account for everything on his order book and his day book was regularly scrutinised by the Clerk of the Union and the findings recorded in the Union minute books.

The master's tasks included the following. To keep a register of all the paupers within the workhouse and to enter the names of those leaving or being admitted to the house. He had to take account of the goods and effects of paupers as they entered the building. He had to provide refreshment and medicines for the sick paupers. He ordered all the food and had to account for all of it and to ensure that there was no waste, and if any product was received of a poor quality he had to report this to the Guardians and the suppliers. He had to inspect all the rooms and wards of the male paupers at least twice a day, and he had to list the faults or misdemeanours of every person in the workhouse and report to the Guardians. He was often asked to punish offenders according to the rule book and enter the name, offence and punishment in the official punishment book. He had to oversee the transit of paupers to the church twice on a Sunday. He and the porter had to ensure that all gates and doors were locked at night, which was at nine o'clock in Winter and ten o'clock in Summer. He also had to arrange the burials of the paupers. On entry to the workhouse the master had to supervise the collection of clothes and the giving out of the workhouse clothing, and also the bathing of the inmate. He also had to give the order to separate the pauper family and direct the members to separate wards or rooms within the workhouse.

The matron or mistress of the house was frequently the wife of the master, as liaison between the two officials was of the paramount importance. Her tasks included the cleanliness of every part of the workhouse and for the management of the kitchen. She had to take care of the bedding and linen and every other article generally under the care of a female. She was expected to visit the rooms and wards of the female paupers twice a day, and to administer medicines to sick paupers and to report to the master any improprieties in the conduct of the paupers. She had to supervise the making of beds every morning, and also the sweeping and cleaning of rooms and corridors. She also had to ensure that the paupers were kept clean.

FORM 15.—The Admission and Discharge Book.

The Admission and Discharge Book kept by the Workhouse Master

FORM 21.—Clothing Receipt Book.

Whence received—from Tradesman, or Clothing Conversion Store.	No. of Invoice.	Folio in Clothing Conversion Book.	**Bedding**			**Men's Clothing**										**Women's Clothing**											**Boys' Clothing**									**Girls' Clothing**										
			Sheets	Blankets	Rugs	Coats	Waistcoats	Trousers	Shirts Linen	Shirts Cotton	Shoes	Stockings	Hats	Handkerchiefs	Gown	Under Petticoats	Upper Petticoats	Shifts Linen	Shifts Cotton	Aprons	Handkerchiefs	Shoes	Stockings	Caps	Bonnet	Coats	Waistcoats	Trousers	Shirts Linen	Shirts Cotton	Shoes	Stockings	Hats	Handkerchiefs	Frocks	Under Petticoats	Upper Petticoats	Shifts Linen	Shifts Cotton	Aprons	Shoes	Stockings	Handkerchiefs	Bonnets

Clothing Receipt Book kept by the Workhouse Master

22

PROVISION RECEIPT and CONSUMPTION ACCOUNT for the   Week of the Quarter ending

			ARTICLES RECEIVED AND ON HAND.				ARTICLES CONSUMED.									
ARTICLES.	Stock in Hand.	Price.	New Stock.	No. of Invoice.	Price.	Cost of New Stock £ s. d.	Total Quantity of Old Stock and New Stock and...	IN THE HOUSE. Quantity	Price	Value £ s. d.	OUT-RELIEF. Quantity	Price	Value £ s. d.	Total Quantity.	Total Value £ s. d.	Remaining in Hand.	Stock required for next Week.

PROVISIONS

Bread	Loaves, 4 lbs.
Flour	Bushels
Meat	lbs.
Cheese	lbs.
Potatoes	Bushels
Peas	qts.
Oatmeal	lbs.
Butter	lbs.
Milk	qts.
Rice	lbs.
Salt	lbs.
Tea	lbs.
Sugar	lbs.
Suet	lbs.

NECESSARIES

Coals	cwts.
Candles	lbs.
Soap	lbs.
Wood	faggots

Folio of Minute Book . .

Folio of Minute Book . .

Folio of Minute Book }

A sheet of this Form out of the Provision Check Account are to be bound up together alternately.

The quantities consumed must correspond with the quantities in the Provision Check Account, and these quantities, with the stock in hand, must equal the total received.

Provision Receipt and Consumption Account kept by the Workhouse Master

Both master and mistress had to supervise the behaviour and work output of the paupers. The attached copy of the rules illustrates clearly the amount of monitoring and discipline that was customary in the workhouse. The tasks set in the house included oakum picking and stone breaking. Oakum picking meant unravelling lengths of rope, and picking all the fibres apart. "Each picker has by his side his weighed quantity òf old rope, cut into lengths about equal to that of a hoop-stick. Some of the pieces are white and sodden looking, whilst others are hard and black with the tar upon them." The air was often full of dust and the hands of the inmates became covered with cuts and blisters. The oakum was then sold and it was subsequently recycled and spun again for ropes and cheap mats. One of the customers of the Bromsgrove workhouse for oakum was the Midland Boat Building Company and in February 1882 the Union offered its product for sale at 22s/6d per cwt. The master also had to supervise stone breaking. This was particularly back breaking work for the able bodied males. The big stones had to be smashed into small particles which were then sold off to private road companies for road surfacing.

One of the first masters of the workhouse was a Mr. Horton whose salary was £50 p.a. He was extremely efficient in his work and despite an increase to £52 p.a. resigned his post in March 1848 and took up a more lucrative post as Master of the Stafford Workhouse. One of the first matrons of the workhouse was a Mrs. Kings, a hard-working, but rather volatile character. Her salary was £30 p.a. Her health and temper seem to have been in a fragile state by August 1848 and she was given a generous fortnights' leave to recover. In November 1848 she and the master were reprimanded for the treatment of Sarah Sadler, a pauper. The nurse was actually dismissed for striking the woman. In September 1853 the redoubtable Mrs. Kings was in trouble again, this time for clashing with Mr. Clarke the master. She accused him of locking her out of the workhouse one night and also of watering the soup. Her claims were found to be without foundation. After this incident Mrs. Kings seems to have stabilised and she continued at her post until she resigned voluntarily in December 1862, having served the union for eighteen years.

The Guardians choice of porters over the years was catastrophic. Most of them were bad characters and added to the stress of the masters. The porters' duties were in the main delegated by the master and involved the reception of paupers and their general welfare. In April 1839 the job of porter was advertised and a William Price was appointed. It was the first of many unwise porter appointments for we read in September 1840 "It having been reported to this Board that Hannah Kirk who for many years past has been an inmate of the workhouse had been delivered of a bastard child since the last meeting of the Board, and it having been stated that the porter was the supposed father of the child - - - - resolved that William Price be forthwith dismissed from this post."

The master of the house was indirectly blamed for the incident in the minutes of October 5th 1840. "It having transpired from the examination of the witnesses in the matter of Hannah Kirk's accusation against William Price the porter that there is a degree of laxity in the discipline of the house - - - - resolved that the governor be admonished by our Chairman, to be more attentive in future."

In July 1847, George White the porter was sacked "for absenting himself from the workhouse without permission and had therefore neglected to perform his duties." In the advertisement for his replacement the Board called for preference to a baker, shoemaker or tailor.

On the 14th June 1859 yet another porter received his cards. Apparently friction had been building up for some time between the porter and the master. "The master of the workhouse reported that Duffill the porter returned to the workhouse about 10 o'clock on the night of the 8th instant, intoxicated with liquor - that he had on other occasions come back drunk and that he sometimes used very bad language to the inmates." Duffill refused to resign and was sacked on the spot by the Guardians. His job was readvertised on a salary of £15 p.a. with preferences given to a baker or tailor. This was not the end of the Duffill incident, for he was a bad tempered man and bent on avenging himself on Clarke the master. He wrote a letter to the Guardians making a number of accusations against him which were ignored by the Board. However, Clarke was obviously rattled by the accusations and tended his resignation along with Miss Cheese the school mistress in August 1859. A Mr. John Rose was appointed as the new master on £50 p.a. two pounds less than his predecessor. A Miss Elizabeth Dance was elected mistress of the workhouse school at a salary of £16 p.a. at the same appointment session. It was soon discovered however, on checking the books that Clarke had consumed one hundred pints of ale which he had not paid for. He was chased by the Board and asked to settle up which he grudgingly did. In the meantime Rose, the new master and Griffin the new porter, didn't get on, and when the master made his first official complaint against Griffin's inefficiency in February 1860 the Board supported it and Griffin was dismissed.

Workhouse Regulations—Punishments, &c.

PUNISHMENT FOR MISBEHAVIOUR OF THE PAUPERS.[2]

Art. 127.—Any pauper, being an inmate of the workhouse, who shall neglect to observe such of the regulations in this Order as are applicable to him as such inmate ;—

Or who shall make any noise when silence is ordered to be kept ;

Or shall use obscene or profane language ;

Or shall by word or deed insult or revile any person ;

Or shall threaten to strike or to assault any person ;

Or shall not duly cleanse his person ;

Or shall refuse or neglect to work, after having been required to do so ;

Or shall pretend sickness ;

Or shall play at cards or other game of chance ;

Or shall refuse to go into his proper ward or yard, or shall enter or attempt to enter, without permission, the ward or yard appropriated to any class of paupers other than that to which he belongs ;

Or shall climb over any fence or boundary wall surrounding any portion of the workhouse premises, or shall attempt to leave the workhouse otherwise than through the ordinary entrance ;

Or shall misbehave in going to, at, or returning from public worship out of the workhouse, or at Divine Service or Prayers in the workhouse ;

Or, having received temporary leave of absence, and wearing the workhouse clothes, shall return to the workhouse after the appointed time of absence, without reasonable cause for delay ;

Or shall wilfully disobey any lawful order of any officer of the workhouse ;

Shall be deemed DISORDERLY.

Art. 128.—Any pauper, being an inmate of the workhouse, who shall, within seven days, repeat any one, or commit more than one, of the offences specified in Art. 127 ;

> Or who shall by word or deed insult or revile the master or matron, or any other officer of the workhouse, or any of the Guardians ;
>
> Or shall wilfully disobey any lawful order of the master or matron, after such order shall have been repeated ;
>
> Or shall unlawfully strike or otherwise unlawfully assault any person ;
>
> Or shall wilfully or mischievously damage or spoil any property whatsoever belonging to the Guardians ;
>
> Or shall wilfully waste or spoil any provisions, stock, tools, or materials for work belonging to the Guardians ;
>
> Or shall be drunk ;
>
> Or shall act or write indecently or obscenely ;
>
> Or shall wilfully disturb other persons at public worship out of the workhouse, or at Divine Service or Prayers in the workhouse ;

Shall be deemed REFRACTORY.

Art. 129.—The master may, with or without the direction of the Guardians, punish any disorderly pauper by substituting during a time not greater than forty-eight hours, for his dinner, as prescribed by the Dietary, a meal consisting of eight ounces of bread, or one pound of cooked potatoes or boiled rice, and also by withholding from him, during the same period, all butter, cheese, tea, sugar, or broth, which such pauper would otherwise receive, at any meal during the time aforesaid.[1]

Art. 130.—The Guardians may, by a special direction to be entered on their minutes, order any refractory pauper to be punished by confinement in a separate room, with or without an alteration of diet, similar in kind and duration to that prescribed in Art. 129 for disorderly paupers ; but no pauper shall be so confined for a longer period than twenty-four hours ; or, if it be deemed right that such pauper should be carried before a justice of the peace, and if such period of twenty-four hours should be insufficient for that purpose ; then for such further time as may be necessary for such purpose.[2]

Art. 131.—If any offence, whereby a pauper becomes refractory, under Art. 128, be accompanied by any of the following circumstances of aggravation (that is to say), if such pauper—

Persist in using violence against any person;

Or persist in creating a noise or disturbance so as to annoy other inmates;

Or endeavour to excite other paupers to acts of insubordination;

Or persist in acting indecently or obscenely in the presence of any other inmate;

Or persist in mischievously breaking or damaging any goods or property of the Guardians;

the master may, without any direction of the Guardians, immediately place such refractory pauper in confinement for any time not exceeding twelve hours; which confinement shall, however, be reckoned as part of any punishment afterwards imposed by the Guardians for the same offence.[1]

Art. 132.—Every refractory pauper shall be deemed to be also disorderly, and may be punished as such; but no pauper who may have been punished for any offence as disorderly shall afterwards be punished for the same offence as refractory, and no pauper who may have been punished for any offence as refractory shall afterwards be punished for the same offence as disorderly.[1]

Art. 133.—No pauper shall be punished by confinement or alteration in diet for any offence not committed in the workhouse since his last admission, except in such cases as are expressly specified in Arts. 127 and 128.

Art. 134.—No pauper who may have been under medical care, or who may have been entered in the medical weekly return as sick or infirm, at any time in the course of the seven days next preceding the punishment, or who may be reasonably supposed to be under twelve or above sixty years of age, or who may be pronounced by the medical officer to be pregnant, or who may be suckling a child, shall be punished by alteration of diet, or by confinement unless the medical officer shall have previously certified in writing that no injury to the health of such pauper is reasonably to be apprehended from the proposed punishment; and any modification diminishing such punishment which the medical officer may suggest shall be adopted by the master.[2]

28

Art. 135.—No pauper shall be confined between eight o'clock in the evening and six o'clock in the morning without being furnished with a bed and bedding suitable to the season, and with the other proper conveniences.

Art. 136.—No child under twelve years of age shall be punished by confinement in a dark room, or during the night.[1]

Art. 137.—No corporal punishment shall be inflicted on any male child, except by the schoolmaster or master.[2]

Art. 138.—No corporal punishment shall be inflicted on any female child.

Art. 139.—No corporal punishment shall be inflicted on any male child, except with a rod or other instrument such as may have been approved of by the Guardians or the Visiting Committee.[3]

Art. 140.—No corporal punishment shall be inflicted on any male child until two hours shall have elapsed from the commission of the offence for which such punishment is inflicted.

Art. 141.—Whenever any male child is punished by corporal correction, the master and schoolmaster shall, if possible, be both present.

Art. 142.—No male child shall be punished by flogging whose age may be reasonably supposed to exceed fourteen years.[4]

Workhouse regulations - punishments.
Punishment for misbehaviour of the paupers

In April 1862 the master and matron were both reprimanded. A complaint was made to the Board by Thomas Portman and his daughter of lice in some of the bedding and clothes. This was proven and both master and mistress were censured. A ruling was made that inmates were to be generally bathed once a month with the consent of the Medical Officer.

On the 9th December 1862 a Mr. and Mrs. Pope, master and schoolmistress of Penkridge Workhouse, were appointed as master and mistress of the Bromsgrove Workhouse. It proved to be a disastrous appointment and brought the Workhouse into chaos, which I have chronicled more fully in the chapter on 'Crises'. In February 1864 the three officials involved in the scandal including Miss Dance, the school mistress, were forced to resign. Seven sets of applications were received for the master and matron posts including one from Mr. Rose who had resigned the post in December 1862. The Guardians again showed their indecision and were not unanimous in their selection. The compromise appointees were Mr. and Mrs. Danks, and a Miss Elizabeth Sheppard was appointed as school mistress on a salary of £20 p.a.

On the third of July 1866 Mr. and Mrs. Danks resigned their posts to enhance their career by seeking promotion in grade to a bigger workhouse. The Board of Guardians placed an advertisement in local newspapers to fill the post.

BROMSGROVE UNION

The election of Master and Matron.

The Guardians of the Bromsgrove Union will, at a meeting to be held on Tuesday, the 17th day of July instant, at half-past eleven o'clock in the forenoon, proceed to the appointment of a master and matron for this workhouse at the respective salaries of £50 and £30 per annum with board, washing and lodging in the house. Preference will be given to a man and his wife without children dependent on them and who have acquired experience from having held similar appointments, and security must be given to the amount of £200 for the faithful performance of their duties. Applications in the handwriting of the parties, stating their respective ages and present and former occupations to be accompanied with testimonials with full particulars of character of a recent date must be forwarded to me on or before Monday the 16th day of July instant. Candidates will be expected to attend at the Union Workhouse on the following day (Tuesday) at half-past eleven o'clock a.m., but no travelling or other expenses can be allowed for such attendance."

By order of the Board
John Humphreys, Clerk
Board Room, Bromsgrove, 3rd July 1866

Mr. and Mrs. Allinson were subsequently appointed at a joint salary of £80 p.a., but almost immediately a letter was received from the Poor Law Board questioning the appointment and the Union was embarrassed to learn that Mr. Allinson, the former master of Ledbury Union, had resigned his post as a result of acrimony with Guardians of that workhouse. The Board, however, stuck to the appointment but there must have been a few red faces amongst them on hearing the news. Mr. Allinson seems to have responded well to his new environment and there were no problems until 1869 and 1870. In March 1869 the Guardians were humiliated by the facts surrounding the death of Eliza Giles, an elderly pauper, who had been transferred to the County Lunatic Asylum in Powick, near Worcester. The death took place within days of her arrival, and the master of the asylum made a vehement attack on the Bromsgrove Guardians for the appearance of the pauper, referring to the bad state of her clothing and her unkempt appearance and that these factors contributed to her death. The Bromsgrove Union disputed this and claimed that she had been well looked after at Bromsgrove. The Poor Law Board appointed an inspector to look into the circumstances and to interview all those concerned, and his report came down heavily against the Bromsgrove Workhouse - - - "that much blame was attributable to the matron and the other officers whose duty it was to see to the cleanliness of her person and prevent her from being actually removed from the workhouse until she was in a fit state to leave it." Mr. and Mrs. Allinson were severely reprimanded by the Guardians for the incident.

In April 1870 the Allinsons received another setback. Joseph Harris, inmate of the workhouse, hanged himself. Dr. Fletcher the MOH for the Workhouse and Bromsgrove District was partly blamed for not having removed Harris at an earlier date to Powick Asylum. By 1875 Mr. Allinson was beginning to show signs of stress and this slowly began to affect his efficiency. Accusations of cruelty were levied against him by a handful of paupers and these claims were supported by the Chaplain. The Board at that stage ignored and dismissed the claims. In August 1876 a more serious charge was made "Selina Yarnold, lately an inmate of the workhouse delivered to the Board a written statement charging the master with ill treatment and cruelty and also with having had improper connections with married women and girls." There was another investigation and once again Allinson was cleared. In November 1876 came the fifth blow caused by the death of a John Lowe, in the tramp ward. Lowe, a vagrant, was found collapsed in Bromsgrove town centre and brought into the workhouse in a cart by a member of the public accompanied by a police officer. The ailing man was received by the porter and placed in the tramp ward, but he should have been placed in the sick ward. The porter's second mistake was not to inform the master of what had happened until it was too late. In the subsequent inquest the master defended himself, "when I went to see him (John Lowe) I saw the man was very ill, so I had him removed to the hospital ward, gave him some brandy, sent for the doctor, but he never rallied." The porter admitted his mistakes and was promptly dismissed, and Allinson was cleared of the charge.

In August 1877 the master faced yet another crisis. Typhoid fever broke out amongst the children of the workhouse. Dr. Carey suggested that the girls should be removed from their ward for one month and that urgent repairs should be done on the sewers. Research revealed that the water from two of the three wells in the workhouse were contaminated and that the water from the pump supplying water from the brook was also polluted. Dr. Carey also linked the outbreak of typhoid to the poor dietary of the children which had lowered their resistance to the dreaded disease and he suggested more butter, bread and milk. As for the contaminated water, nothing could be done until 1884 when the workhouse at last was able to get clean drinking water from the newly established 'East Worcestershire Waterworks Company'.

By September 1877 Allinson's health had deteriorated and on the 11th instant it was revealed that his weekly totals of expenses did not tally (for the first time in eleven years). The Guardians were horrified by the lapse, and they received an apology from the master and an explanation for the mistakes. He also sent a letter to the Guardians asking for two months leave from work, and his request was supported by a medical certificate. However, most Guardians were unsympathetic to the man's distress and criticised the state of the workhouse "in going round the house, they found it to be in a very unsatisfactory state and things were neglected, and that the master appeared to be unable to discharge his duties." Several Guardians proposed that he should resign! The stunned Allinson asked for a few weeks to recover from his illness, but by a vote of 6 to 5 he was asked to resign. He and his wife resigned their posts on September 11th 1877. Adverts were placed in the local press for replacements and then the Guardians suddenly suffered the pangs of conscience for the appalling way they had treated Allinson and the order to resign was rescinded. Alas! fate was against him for the Local Government Board intervened and overruled the Board decreeing that Allinson's letter of resignation had been received and that was the end of the matter. His resignation therefore had to stand! Such was the reward for eleven years of loyalty to the Bromsgrove Union.

Eleven sets of applications were received for the vacant posts; once again the Guardians were split on the choice of candidates. Mr. and Mrs. John Booth of Bromsgrove were eventually appointed and almost immediately another controversy began. The Local Government Board intervened once again and blocked the appointment - - - "the Board could not feel satisfied that Mr. and Mrs. Booth were fit persons for such important office, and observed that neither of them had had any experience in any branch of the Poor Law Administration or any other public service, and that Mr. Booth was then a bankrupt person!"

The Bromsgrove Board still reeling from the Allinson debacle were deeply embarrassed by this revelation which so clearly showed their own incompetence. The Guardians opposed the ruling and a compromise solution was eventually agreed upon - the Booths were to be given a three months trial. The Booths only lasted two months for in December 1878 certain deficiencies were found in the stores especially in the quantity of brandy!

Sixteen sets of applications were received for the vacancies and a Mr. and Mrs. Leaton were appointed in February 1878 on a salary of £60 and £30 respectively, and this time the LGB ratified the appointment. However, within six months friction had built up between the porter and the master and on the 10th July 1878 the porter resigned after Mr. Leaton "found a woman in the porter's bed at 10.00 p.m. after the workhouse was locked up." The wise Guardians then decided to advertise for a married couple to do the porter and cook's jobs. It was stressed that the porter should be able to read and write and that the cook should also assist the matron in general duties. Mr. and Mrs. Barnard of Birmingham were appointed on a salary of £16 p.a. and £14 p.a. respectively - sadly friction quickly built up amongst the four personalities within weeks. Barnard was caught by the master stealing workhouse meat - this incident and others caused Leaton to remark "that he and his wife had quite made up their minds to resign their appointments rather than longer submit to the insolence of the porter and the cook." The Guardians pacified the master and demanded the resignation of the porter and as a result the Barnards soon departed. Mr. Barnard later wrote to the Board smearing the character of the master but all the claims were dismissed as malicious gossip. The Leatons continued in office until September 1881 when they moved on to another workhouse.

A new master named Wyatt was appointed, and in 1883 a clash of personalities took place between him and the newly appointed 'Superintendent of Labour', Mr. Adolphus Browning. The latter was in charge of setting profitable work to the pauper inmates and arranging the sale of these products such as oakum, stone and firewood. The confrontation came when Browning accused Wyatt of stealing some of the money for the sale of firewood. Wyatt claimed not to have received the money and the amount was not credited in his books. The Guardians eventually accepted the master's explanation that he had received the sum, but had simply forgotten about it due to pressures of work. He was severely censured and was instructed to repay the missing payment of £8 - 1s - 2d out of his own pocket. After this incident the house settled down to a period of stability once again until the 16th October 1889 when typhoid fever broke out in the workhouse and claimed its only victim - poor Mr. Wyatt. His death caused a panic amongst the Guardians and the drains and sewers were checked and cleaned.

The posts for a new master and matron were advertised in the regional press and drew 23 applications, and a Mr. and Mrs. Owen from Stow-on-Wold workhouse were elected on October 19th 1889. The couple did an efficient job and on the 23rd June 1891 they tended their resignation and took up another similar appointment, but at a larger workhouse at Wakefield, Yorkshire. Twenty-one married couples applied for the vacancy, and thirteen couples were invited for interview. Mr. and Mrs. Barrows were duly elected at salaries of £60 and £30 respectively and they stayed at the Bromsgrove Workhouse until July 1900 when they left to take up similar posts at the Stratford-upon-Avon Workhouse.

The Barrows had a fairly untroubled stay at Bromsgrove and were involved only in one incident. The episode in question happened in October 1894 when the master reported Mr. Grove, the Labour Master, for being insolent to the matron and for general neglect of duty. Mr. Grove "admitted that he was insolent to the matron and should not care if he was again as she was a mischief maker and considered he should be instructed by the master and not the matron." The Board asked him for his resignation. However within a few days Mr. Grove had repented and notified the Guardians that he wished to retain his post and that he had apologised to the Board for the way he had spoken to the Board at the last meeting. The master and matron were called in and both agreed that Mr. Grove had offered a suitable apology. The resolution calling for the Labour Master to resign was rescinded and he was allowed to continue in office.

The Guardians were well pleased with the service record of Mr. and Mrs. Barrows and gave the couple a glowing testimonial - - - "that in the opinion of this Board, Mr. and Mrs. Barrows possess many qualities fitting them for the positions they hold and the Guardians are glad to know that they leave Bromsgrove to enter upon a greater sphere of usefulness and responsibility in the management of a larger workhouse."

In early February 1900 a Mr. and Mrs. Nowell were appointed as the new master and matron of the Bromsgrove Union.

The duty of the Medical Officer of Health was also a stressful occupation. In November 1836 the twelve union parishes were divided into four medical areas, each with a medical officer. The medical officer for the Bromsgrove district was also the medical officer of the workhouse and he received £70 p.a. The medical officer for the Belbroughton area received £50 p.a. and the officers for the Tardebigge and Alvechurch districts received £40 p.a. each.

In May 1837 Dr. Kendrick, the first MOH for Bromsgrove was forced to resign after falsifying some documentation on an ailing pauper; and James Bruce died as a result of the neglect of the doctor. Dr. Fletcher was appointed the new MOH for Bromsgrove and he too almost lost his job in July 1847 when he claimed expenses from the Union for visiting a patient, which was an untruth. Dr. Fletcher retained his job and became one of the hardest working members of the Union, and served the area for thirty-five loyal years retiring eventually on the 29th October 1872.

The MOH was also indirectly accountable after March 1837 to the newly created national system of the 'Registry of Births and Deaths'. In May 1839 a nurse was appointed at £6 p.a. to help nurse the sick in the workhouse and she worked closely with the MOH. In January 1842 the death of the indoor pauper Henry Cartright took place in the workhouse, and Dr. Fletcher was admonished by the Board. I have detailed this incident in the chapter entitled 'Crises'.

Many epidemics broke out in the area in the nineteenth century and the four MOH's had to work excessively hard on these occasions. They also had to fight against the ignorance of the local populace who had a detestation of new medical practices such as vaccination. One of the main killers was smallpox and despite the successful work of Edward Jenner in 1798 and the introduction of vaccination, ordinary people were full of fear and many refused to be vaccinated because they thought they would assume the features of a cow. This ignorance was caused by the fact that Jenner's vaccination was associated with cowpox. Other diseases included the dreaded cholera which in 1849 in London killed off during its peak 2000 people a week, and killed 53,000 in England and Wales, 7000 in Scotland and 30,000 in Ireland. In 1832 cholera had killed 50,000 people including fifty townspeople of Redditch.   Cholera was primarily caused by contaminated drinking water and the generally filthy conditions of most towns and cities of the period.   Typhus, measles, scarlet fever were other killers found in our area.

On January 11th 1841, typhoid fever broke out in Bromsgrove and caused widespread panic.   In November 1842 measles broke out in the workhouse and family visits were suspended until the outbreak was over.   On January 23rd 1843 typhus fever broke out in Redditch "which was attributed to the many nuisances arising from decayed animal and vegetable matter, stagnant water etc., which exist there." In September 1843 there was an attack of typhus and diarrhoea in Bromsgrove and Alvechurch and also in the workhouse, and even some of the Guardians suffered.   The drains were found to be the cause.   On the 17th May 1847 typhus broke out in the workhouse, and Mary Gibbs, inmate was isolated with a nurse in a special ward.   The nurse, Sarah Pugh of Bromsgrove, had only just been appointed to serve the Union on a salary of £15 p.a.   Both nurse and patient survived the plague.   Cholera ravaged the nation and the local area in 1849 and there were many deaths (see chapter on 'Crises').   In November 1850 cholera returned and killed Thomas Hodgetts aged 75 in Catshill, Bromsgrove; the cause was "an offensive privy used by fifty persons."   In January 1851 there was a smallpox epidemic in Droitwich and Dr. Fletcher was very much afraid of it coming to the locality. Some six hundred persons were unvaccinated in the Board's area, and Fletcher had a tremendous task on his hands in reasoning with the gullible and ignorant mass that vaccination would save their lives; not turn them into cows.   Fletcher worked unceasingly to vaccinate the public and in March 1851 the Board begrudgingly agreed to the increase in vaccination fees payable to him from 1s-3d to 1s-6d a case.   In September and October smallpox and typhoid ravaged Redditch and Webheath, and again many inhabitants refused to be vaccinated and some had to be threatened with the withdrawal of outdoor relief if they did not comply.   By December 1851 the smallpox epidemic reached a peak and claimed victims amongst the ranks of the unvaccinated.   In January 1852 smallpox returned to Bromsgrove and again in 1863 where it claimed one victim.   In March 1864 smallpox was prevalent in Droitwich and extended to Wychbold and Tardebigge.   In April 1869 scarlet fever and measles were found in Catshill and Sidemoor.

The 'Vaccination Act' of 1867 made vaccinations compulsory, but Dr. Fletcher continued to complain about the ignorance and fear amongst the people.   In February

1871 he was quoted in the minute book "a great number of children in the union had not been vaccinated and were unprotected from smallpox which was so fatal in London and other places and must ere long reach this neighbourhood and Dr. Fletcher suggested that notices should be sent to the parents of children not vaccinated threatening proceedings - ordered that the registrars be required to have their lists of defaulters ready by the next meeting." In March smallpox broke out in Feckenham, and in May it broke out at Stoke Works, Bromsgrove. In February 1872 the smallpox broke out in Redditch where there was widespread panic, and all four MOH were kept very busy.

In October 1872 Dr. Fletcher's thirty five years as MOH of Bromsgrove came to an end and he retired. He was succeeded by Dr. Charles Davenport who sadly died in January 1875 before making an impression on the job. He was succeeded by Dr. Charles Carey who was appointed at a salary of £90 p.a. thirty pounds for duties as medical officer of the workhouse and sixty pounds for his duties as medical officer of the Bromsgrove district. He was also to be paid a rate of 1s-6d for each case of successful vaccination in the Bromsgrove district including the workhouse. On the 14th August 1877 typhoid fever broke out amongst the children of the workhouse. Contaminated water was the cause and Dr. Carey also associated the illness with a poor dietary and he suggested more bread, butter and milk should be given to the girls.

In January 1878 the Bromsgrove Cottage Hospital opened and the secretary of the hospital invited the work-house to send patients and also asked the Guardians for financial contributions. The Guardians gave him a cool reception and shortly afterwards started planning for a hospital wing in the workhouse complex, which was completed in September 1885 to hold 68 beds (31 men and 31 women and 6 lying in ward). In the meantime measles and scarlet fever had broken out in the workhouse in November 1881, and in the town of Bromsgrove in February 1882.

In February 1883 Dr. Carey asked for a salary increase and got it. News of his rise spread and Mr. William Smith, MOH for Redditch also asked for an increase in March 1883 claiming that his salary had remained unchanged at £40 p.a. since 1843 when the town's population was a mere 5,000 people, and that it was now a town of 10,000 people; the inference being that his wages should therefore be doubled. The Board curtly dismissed his case and offered no rise in wages!

In October 1888 Dr. Carey resigned his post and gave the Guardians a strange reason for leaving "having decided on leaving Bromsgrove in consequence of the place not suiting my son's health." He was replaced by Dr. Kidd.

Typhoid returned to the area, attacking the workhouse in July 1887 and October 1889 and killed Mr. W. Wyatt the master on the 16th October. Shortly after the opening of the new workhouse hospital, and in answer to a criticism levied at the Board by an inspector of the Local Government Board, another nurse was appointed by the name of Miss Mary Brant, a certified and highly competent nurse who had done her training at the Fever Hospital, Leicester. All the fourteen Guardians in the board room voted for her and she accepted the £25 p.a. post. At the same time, in March 1886 a master's assistant was appointed at £20 p.a. This was a newly created post and included helping the master and also seeing the vagrants and acting as Superintendent for Labour.

The Medical Officer of Health's job was an extremely demanding one and one which was not very well paid. The job description involved three duties; firstly he carried out duties as MOH for the Bromsgrove district; secondly he was the Medical officer for the workhouse and thirdly he was also the public vaccinator for the area. When Dr. Carey was appointed he was paid a total of £130 p.a. Dr. Kidd who replaced him in October 1888 was dissatisfied with his salary by 1891 and wrote the following letter to the Board on the 17th January 1891.

"Mr. Chairman and Gentlemen,

At the commencement of this, the third year of my work in connection with the Bromsgrove District I am constrained to ask you to refix my salary at the figure allowed to my predecessor Dr. Carey if not to raise it. At the time of my appointment I was altogether unaware of the very large proportion of pauperism which exists in this district, but from a table which has come into my hands, I find that in the seven years 1876-1882 the number of patients actually treated in the district steadily increased from 321 to 888 and in the present condition of the staple trade of the place (a reference to the decline in the fortune of the Bromsgrove nailing industry) I have no doubt that this increase has continued. In the year just ended with influenza and two widespread epidemics of measles I can safely say that I have performed the work in the district at a pecuniary loss to myself. The aggregate salary paid to Dr. Carey was £130; £90 for the district and £40 for the work-house as compared with £80 and £30 received by me.

38

I would not object to continue the workhouse attendance at the present salary, but the hardship lies in the district work and I would suggest that a fair way of returning to the previous aggregate of £130 would be to raise the present salary of £80 for the district to £100 leaving the salary for the workhouse at £30."

Dr. Kidd was quite correct in claiming that his salary was lower than his predecessor, but omitted to include the lucrative revenue he was getting (in addition to his salary) for his duties as public vaccinator. He was paid in the region of 1s-6d per vaccination.

The Board took a dim view of his letter, and his manner; and his request for a salary increase was turned down. The Board also mentioned his additional income from his duty as public vaccinator.

On the 6th February 1891 the indignant Dr. Kidd replied by letter and said that he wished to resign the post of District Medical Officer, but he wished to continue in the posts of public vaccinator and medical officer for the workhouse. This reply only hardened the attitude of the Board and they replied by letter accepting his resignation but also demanding that he relinquish the other two appointments as well!

This letter put the fear of God into the unfortunate Kidd as he realised that he had gambled and lost all. He had now made a number of enemies amongst the Guardians and a smear campaign against him suddenly appeared in the "Bromsgrove Messenger."

Dr. Kidd responded valiantly to the circumstances in his letter to the Board dated 21st February 1891 - - - - "I have read with some astonishment the remarks by various members of the Board in the discussion which terminated in the passing of this resolution and which are made public in the 'Messenger'. - - - - - It still seems to me to have been an eminently reasonable request of mine by no means deserving of the epithets "curt" and "cool" applied to it by one gentleman and "dictation" applied to it by another - - - -. It is true that in this particular district it has hitherto happened that the same man has held the three appointments but there is no necessity that this should be so and in many other unions the appointments are held by different men - - -. The Board would make it appear that I have treated them badly. I will venture to say that during the two years in which I have held office under them no official has served them more faithfully - - -. I am willing to leave to the public the question on which side the ungenerous treatment lies. I must respectfully decline to resign the appointment of Public Vaccinator and Medical Officer to the Workhouse unless compelled to do so by order of the Government Board." This last remark angered the Board even more as the Guardians believed it was an attempt to belittle them and bypass their ruling by going directly to the Local Government Board. Dr. Kidd's post-script memo' at the base of his letter set the cat amongst the pigeons. - - - - "I am told since writing the above that a chief factor in determining the refusal of my request was the fact that I did not solicit privately the support of individual members of the Board!"

The Guardians were incensed by this cutting remark and almost immediately dismissed him without waiting for his appeal to be processed by the Local Government Board. They appointed a Dr. Edgar Elliott as Medical Officer of the Bromsgrove district at a salary of £80 p.a.

However, Dr. Kidd was soon to be vindicated for part of his actions. He obviously knew his rights as an employee, as the letter dated the 17th March 1891 from the Local Government Board was to prove. Part of their reply went as follows - - - - "As regards the remarks contained in your letter I am directed to state that the Board would not be prepared to require Mr. Kidd's resignation of the office of District Medical Officer. The two offices are entirely distinct and the officer is entitled to hold each of them upon the terms of the regulations applicable to such office. As to Mr. Kidd's appointment as Public Vaccinator I am directed to point out that the contract entered into with him in that capacity contains a provision under which it can be terminated by either party on 28 days notice." The Board were dismayed by the ruling but immediately put the termination of Dr. Kidd's contract into its 28 days finality. Dr. Kidd, pleased with the letter from the L.G.B. wrote a letter to the Guardians still hoping to placate and win support for his case. He made a plea that he should continue with the two posts of Public Vaccinator and Workhouse Medical Officer. However, the obstinate Board has made up its mind, and with the bit frimly between its teeth pressed on by giving him 28 days notice of dismissal from the post of Public Vaccinator. Dr. Elliott, quick to fill the vacuum, told the Board that he was eager and willing to apply for the forthcoming vacancy. The petulant Guardians accepted the man's offer and appointed him as the new Public Vaccinator. Having put Dr. Kidd in his place they allowed him to continue with just the one post, that of Workhouse Medical Officer.

The furtive Dr. Elliott who capitalised on a fellow doctor's misfortune was soon to ask for a rise in wages. In April 1892 the Board refused his request but gave him £20 as an honorarium in consideration of his extra duties during a recent influenza epidemic. Dissatisfied with this he sent a letter to the Board on the 10th October 1893 "to terminate the appointments of District Medical Officer and Public Vaccinator as he finds them unremunerative." A Dr. Richard Wood was appointed in his place. Before his departure Dr. Elliott did have to respond to a small outbreak of smallpox in the town of Bromsgrove. Three men suffered from it and were moved quickly to Kings Norton Hospital.

Dr. Wood received a salary increase in March 1896 and this was increased again in June 1896 from £80 to £100 p.a. The Union was afraid of an outbreak of smallpox in April, because the epidemic had already struck Gloucester. However, their fears were in vain and the dreaded illness failed to appear in Bromsgrove.

The year 1896 was to be an eventful medical year for another reason, and involved the appointment of a nurse named Ellen Burnstead. She was appointed in January 1896 to replace Rebecca Barnett who gave up her position after just two weeks due to the hard work associated with the job including working at nights. Miss Burnstead was appointed "at a salary of £30 p.a. with board, Lodging and Washing and one month's notice to terminate the appointment on either side." Nurse Burnstead soon became unpopular because of her stern and regimented ways and on the 19th May two inmates complained to the Board. She was called before the Board "and informed of the complaints and asked to try and make matters more pleasant." She was reported again in June and accused of being too harsh and of punishing an improving female patient by forcing her to stay in bed contrary to the orders of the doctor. Dr. Kidd, however, tried to save her career - - - "he thought that the inmate did not yet understand her. He thought the unkindness spoken of was due to the fact that she was enforcing greater discipline and order in the Infirmary than had hitherto been the case. His orders had always been carried out and he considered the nurse an excellent officer and trusted the Board would support her." The Board ignored Dr. Kidd's plea and asked for her resignation on the 16th June 1896. Miss Burnstead ignored the Board, and she had to be reminded a second time before she finally resigned her post on the 14th July. She was then asked to leave the building within 48 hours and given a month's salary. The assistant nurse resigned in November 1896 complaining of the hard work involved in the workhouse.

Another local hospital had opened its doors in 1895 to supplement the workhouse hospital and the Bromsgrove

Cottage Hospital. This was the Smallwood Hospital in Redditch. It was founded by the generosity of two brothers, Edwin and William Smallwood who came from a wealthy local needle-making family. When Edwin died he left a sum of £70,000 and instructed that £5,000 be used for the founding of Redditch Hospital. William Smallwood also donated towards the building of the Cottage Hospital. The hospital was built in the centre of Redditch and took less than two years to build for the cost of £20,000. There were three main wards and two side wards and accommodated thirty beds.

In May 1896 the Guardians received a letter from the Secretary of the Smallwood Hospital stating that a pauper patient named Ann Hemmington had been removed to the hospital suffering from a fractured leg and asking that some allowance be made towards her maintenance. The Board responded "carried that the outdoor relief allowance of 3/- per week be stopped and that such amount be paid to the hospital during the detention of the patient."

The legislation associated with the forthcoming National Insurance Act of 1911 was to alleviate such costs and shame to some extent. However the real thrust of the Welfare State in the direction of hospital treatment did not begin until 1948.

The post of collector of the poor rates, of which there were three in the Union in 1865 was a demanding and unpopular one, the collector often regarded as an ogre. On collection, the money was deposited in a local bank, and then redistributed to care for both indoor and out relief. In November 1867 the Board of Guardians advertised the post of collector of poor rates for the townships of Redditch and Webheath - - - - "the salary will be £52 p.a. and the person appointed will be required to give a bond in the penal sum of £300 in the names of himself and two sufficient sureties, for the due and faithful performance of the duties of the office as to the Township of Redditch, and a like security for £100 as the township of Webheath." The post was one requiring honesty, integrity and tact, and was fraught with temptation for the weak willed, hence the large bonds in both instances.

There were three relieving officers on the books on the Union in 1865. The task of the relieving officer was to visit the needy, report the cases to the Board, and when sanctioned he then paid outrelief to the successful applicants. The unsuccessful applicants had no option but to seek indoor relief, i.e. the workhouse. Sometimes the outrelief was paid in money and at other times in kind such as bread. Sometimes the Board gave loans to the needy and a contract had to be signed by the recipient. The relieving officer therefore often faced temptation in his work, and had to give a bond and surety in the form of a big deposit of money to the union on his appointment.

The relieving officers had to keep a record of all monies and the names of the out paupers, and they had to deliver these records to the Union for frequent scrutiny. Every penny had to be accounted for.

Sadly, Walter Bladon, the relieving officer for the Redditch district fell foul of the Board on the 28th April 1874. His was a tragic story. He failed to send his books for examination, the first failure in seventeen years. He was ordered to appear in front of the Board where he confessed "he had not paid the poor of Redditch and Webheath the relief in money to which they were entitled last week, having applied the money in payment of a debt owing by him." He appeared in the boardroom in a highly distressed state and poured out his profuse apologies for what had happened. He admitted that the cause of his demise was an embarrassing situation which had been going on for about 14 years, and that he had expected that his financial circumstances would have improved by the previous week. He blamed a friend for not repaying the money in time - - - -. He expressed his deep regret that he had made default in paying the poor and placed himself entirely in the hands of the Board."

Mr. Bladon, full of remorse also wrote a begging letter to the Local Government Board claiming that he had served as relieving officer for 17 years without a complaint against him and could the Board forgive him for this episode. Surprisingly, and out of character, the Board exercised mercy and forgave him and allowed him to keep his position. This certainly would not have happened in the early years of the Bromsgrove Workhouse Union. He was cautioned and instructed to repay all the money in instalments.

The Guardians must have also realised that a contributory factor in the incident was his low wages, much lower than his counterpart in the Bromsgrove district, for they increased his wages to £80 p.a., and in February 1875 they increased the wages again to £90 p.a.

His suspension of three months was ended and he was allowed to continue with his work and his first task was to get "a warrant for the apprehension of William Griffiths, late of Redditch, engine driver, for running away and leaving his wife and two small children, they having become chargeable to the common fund of this Union." Such tasks were very much part of the work of the relieving officer in workhouse England in Victorian times. Having, seemingly, recovered from this financial mess, Walter Bladon's fortunes progressed well until the early 1880's when he again faltered. Suffering badly from rheumatism he found it increasingly difficult to do his work and his end was a very tragic and self-inflicted one. His body was recovered from the Birmingham and Worcester canal at Tardebigge in September 1882. When his books were checked by the Board they were found to contain a number of inaccuracies.

All successive relieving officers seem to have done their work efficiently until the appearance of Mr. Potter, who looked after the Catshill district of Bromsgrove. He emerges from the minute books as quite a character, who loved his 'tipple'. He first appears in November 1893 when several paupers complained that he had not distributed relief to them to their homes. He was severely admonished by the Board and given a last chance. Yet, on the 16th January the Guardians appointed him as school attendance officer for Belbroughton at an additional £15 p.a. Mr. Potter was reprimanded yet again in June 1894 for refusing to give relief to a pauper, but allowed to continue with his work. In January 1895 he was reported to the Board by Mr. R. Smallwood, a local J.P., for failure to complete some documentation "and he was not sober at the time." It looked as if the axe of dismissal would surely fall on the likeable Potter. The repentent Potter wrote a begging letter to the Guardians on the 14th January 1895.

"I beg to express my sincere regret for the unfortunate condition in which I appeared at the last Board meeting (he was intoxicated at the time!) I was prevailed upon to attend a social gathering of a few friends the previous evening, with the result that I took too much. My remorse since has been most sincere. I know that the Board have already been very kind and most indulgent to me and that I have no claim upon you for further forgiveness, but I appeal to your mercy and beg for a last and final chance of saving my character. If my appeal to the clemency of the Board is not in vain I will give you an assurance that I will, for the future, become a total abstainer - - - - - - .

I am Ladies and Gentlemen,
Your repentent and humble servant,
R.E. Potter"

The Chaplain of the workhouse had many onerous duties and the pay was low. Usually the Chaplain was also a full time cleric in the area and it was frequently seen that his conflicting duties clashed. The Chaplain's views carried a lot of weight with the Guardians, and his recommendations were nearly always followed. In December 1853 the Board accepted his recommendations that a supply of bibles and testaments be provided for the use of the inmates of the workhouse and that 20 cassocks be made and placed in the workhouse chapel; that 5s-6d be allowed to the chaplain to purchase books for prizes to be given to the most deserving children. In April 1854 the Chaplain's request for twelve additional prayer books for the use of the inmates, and that a bible should be kept in each ward was accepted.

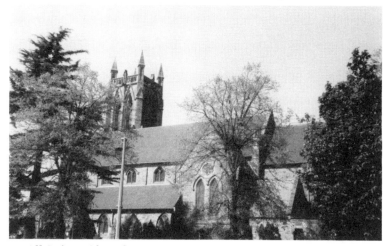

All Saints Church, Bromsgrove. In May 1896 the Vicar invited three workhouse boys to join the church choir.

In September 1857 the Chaplain, the Reverend Aldham resigned due to the pressures of the workhouse. Obviously he was a busy man with other responsibilities outside the workhouse and he had frequently sent deputies to cover his workhouse duties, and this practice had incurred the displeasure of the Guardians. His resignation left the Board with a major headache, for when the advertisement appeared in the local press not one application was received. In consequence of this the paupers were given permission to attend services at the parish church. The men and boys were put in the care of the master and porter and the women and girls were chaperoned by the matron and schoolmistress. This inconvenience was rectified on the 15th June 1858, nine months after the departure of the Reverend Aldham. The Reverend Charles Day accepted the post at a salary of £40 a year. He stayed at the post until the 25th September 1858 and was replaced by the Reverend George Turner Tatham. He resigned in May 1859 on his appointment as headmaster of Preston Grammar School. His successor, the Reverend Kingdom didn't last long either and he left on the 15th September 1860 to become master of the lower sixth class in King's College School, London. The Reverend Hoare was appointed as the next Chaplain. The Board of Guardians considered themselves as God-fearing men and were staunch members of the established church, and in May 1864 they made a determined stand against the Roman Catholic 'influences' - - - - "resolved that a petition be sent to the House of Commons against the admission of Roman Catholic chaplains and the celebration of the mass in Union workhouses."

There was always a harmonious association between the Union and the local vicar. An example of this is seen in May 1896 "a letter was received from the Vicar of All Saints stating if the Guardians will permit he should like two or three of the workhouse boys to join the choir at All Saints. It was resolved that the Vicar be thanked for his letter and informed that the Board be pleased for the boys to attend."

The Clerk of the Bromsgrove Union held a most important post, and his salary reflected this stature. In December 1891 a vacancy arose, and the full time post was advertised at £175 p.a. His role included; the keeping of the minute books for the Bromsgrove Union, the checking of the books of the relieving officers and also the Master's 'Day Book' and 'Receipt and Payment Book'. He was also clerk to the Assessment Committee, Rural Sanitary Authority and School Attendance Committee. In addition it was his task to compile all medical returns. Two men were invited to interview from the original list of seven applications; Mr. Parry, a nail manufacturer from Bromsgrove and Mr. Holloway, Assistant Clerk to the Guardians of the Stourbridge Union. After an intense competition the latter was appointed in January 1892. The breakdown of his salary was as follows:-

Clerk to the Guardians	— £100 p.a.
School Attendance Committee Clerk	— £ 25 p.a.
Rural Sanitary Authority Clerk	— £ 25 p.a.
Clerk to the Assessment Committee	— £ 25 p.a.
Total	£175 p.a.

The work of the clerk had almost doubled since the opening of the workhouse in 1838 and his authority now applied to sixteen parishes and townships; Alvechurch, Belbroughton, Bentley Pauncefoot, Bromsgrove, Clent, Cofton Hackett, Frankley, Grafton Manor, Hagley, Hunnington, Pedmore, Redditch, Romsley, Stoke Prior, Tutnall and Cobley, and Webheath.

46

Mr. Holloway's minutes are extremely orderly and well-kept and even more informative than those of his predecessor. We learn that in the fortnight ending on the 19th January 1892 there were 113 cases for outdoor relief and that there were 192 paupers in the 350 pauper-sized institution. In addition an average of 103 vagrants per week had been relieved in the period, and that there were 82 lunatics in the Powick Asylum. We also learn that there were many deaths from influenza in the first two weeks of January 1892. By late February the weather and influenza had eased and we discover that in the two week period ending on the 1st March 1892 that 96 had been given outdoor relief; that there were 150 paupers in the workhouse. By the fortnight ended on the 19th July 1892 the following figures applied; outdoor relief was granted to 46 cases; there were only 112 paupers actually in the workhouse; a hundred vagrants had been relieved on average per week and the number of lunatics at Powick chargeable to the Union amounted to eighty-four.

In concluding this particular chapter I have focused attention on the Guardians themselves. All were men of property and standing in the community and were elected for a term of office. The illustration depicts the results of such elections in 1898. The Guardians were blindly obedient to the doctrine of the New Poor Law in the early years and not until the 1870's were there any signs of a more relaxed and caring attitude towards pauperism in our area.

The relationship between Guardians and appointed and salaried officers of the Union was always very formal and businesslike. Failings were punished by instant dismissal in the early years, and staff who asked for increases in salary were unsuccessful and often incurred the wrath of the Guardians.

Their attitude was conservative and anti-change and they opposed any measure that would eventually increase the local rates. They opposed the 1870 Education Act and were reticent in giving financial aid to parents to enable them to pay the school fees to Board Schools. Documents which did not interest them were often ignored or put on one side until the matter became pressing e.g. "Circular letters were read from the Gateshead and Peterborough Unions on the subject of the Education Bill of 1896 - ordered to lie on the table" and in December 1898 - - - "Papers were received from the parliamentary committee dealing with the question of Old Age Pensions - - - ordered to lie on the table."

The Guardians were loyal to the government and especially to the Royal family, and they behaved in a more relaxed manner towards the paupers in their charge on special royal occasions. On Queen Victoria's Jubilee in June 1897 which celebrated the monarch's sixty years as Queen of the Realm a festive week was held in Bromsgrove. The Guardians decreed that in honour of the event all outdoor paupers would receive two shillings extra relief for that week, and that indoor paupers would receive extra allowances of tobacco, sugar, fruits, biscuits and sweets.

NOTICE OF
RESULT OF ELECTIONS
BROMSGROVE UNION.

ELECTION of GUARDIANS for the above-named Union in the Year 1898

I, the undersigned, being the Returning Officer at the election of Guardians for the said Union hereby give notice that the Candidates whose names are entered in Column 6 of the Statement hereupon opposite to the names of Parishes in which polls have been taken, have been declared duly elected Guardians I hereby declare that the Persons whose names are entered in the said column (or in Column 7) opposite to names of Parishes where no polls have been taken were duly elected (or are to be deemed re-elected) Guardians for the same.

Parishes	Candidates		Places of Abode	Number of Votes recorded	Names of Candidates elected	Names of retiring Guardians deemed to be re-elected
1	Surnames 2	Other Names 3	4	5	6	7
BROMSGROVE	LEWIS	Henry William	Rock Hill, Bromsgrove	552	LEWIS, Henry William	
	LEADBETTER	Job	Melbourne House, Station Street, Bromsgrove	647	LEADBETTER, Job	
	BOWEN	George	Stoney Hill, Bromsgrove	246		
	HALL	Robert Anthony	110, High Street, Bromsgrove	593	HALL, Robert Anthony	
	TILT	Joseph	Birmingham Road, Bromsgrove	205		
	WEDLEY	James	Sheepcote	191		
NORTH BROMSGROVE	SCOTT	Amelia	The Uplands, Green Hill, Bromsgrove	160		
	STEVENSON	David Robert	Chadwich Manor, Bromsgrove	127	STEVENSON, David Robert	
	BOTT	Thomas	New House, Catshill	100	BOTT, Thomas	
	BENNIE	William Struthers	Dodford	59		
	WEAVER	Thomas	Townsend Farm, Bromsgrove	169	WEAVER, Thomas	
REDDITCH	NEASOM	William	Birchensale Farm, North Redditch		NEASOM, William	
	PLAYFAIR	Charlotte	The Cedars, Redditch		PLAYFAIR, Charlotte	
	ALLCOCK	Jane	The Cedars, Redditch		ALLCOCK, Jane	

Dated this 5th day of April, 1898.

H. D. HOLLOWAY,
Returning Officer.

Printed and Published by Messrs Ebrington & Co. Market Place, Bromsgrove

Poster declaring the result of an election for Guardians

1.—*Number and Constituency of Guardians.*

1. The number of the Guardians shall be nineteen; of which number five shall be elected for the parish of Bromsgrove; three for the parish of Tardebigg; and one for each of the other parishes in the Union.

2. But the same person may be elected Guardian for more than one parish, agreeably to Sec. 40 of the Poor Law Amendment Act.

II.—*Duration of the Office.*

The Guardians first elected will continue in Office until the day hereinafter appointed for the annual election of Guardians, and thenceforward the said office shall be held for one year; but the same person who may have been a Guardian for any past year may be re-elected a Guardian for any ensuing year.

III.—*Qualification of Guardians.*

Any person who shall be rated to the poor-rate in some parish in the Union, in respect of hereditaments, of the annual value or rental of not less than Twenty-five pounds, and who, within two years next previous to the day of election, shall not have been dismissed from any office in any parish or Union by order of the Poor Law Commissioners, shall be eligible as a Guardian for any of the said parishes.

IV.—*Qualification of Voters for Guardians, and Scale of Votes.*

1. Any rate payer who shall have been rated to the poor rate in any parish in the Union for the whole year immediately preceding his voting, and shall have paid the parochial rates and assessments made on him for one whole year, as well as those due from him, at the time of voting, except those which have been made or become due within the six months immediately preceding such voting, will be entitled, on the election of the Guardian or Guardians for such parish, to the number and proportion of votes specified in Sec. 40 of the Poor Law Amendment Act; that is to say,—

If he be rated or assessed at any sum under 200l. .... } be will have 1 vote.

If he be rated or assessed at 200l. but under 400l. .... } he will have 2 votes.

And if rated or assessed at 400l. or upwards .... } he will have 3 votes.

2. Any owner of rateable property, situate within any such parish, who shall have given to one of the churchwardens and overseers thereof, on any day previous to the day on which he shall claim to vote, a statement, in writing, of his name and address, and the description of the property in the parish or place, as owner whereof he claims to vote, will be entitled to have the same number and proportion of votes, on the election of the Guardian or Guardians for such parish as is provided for inhabitants and other persons by the Parish Vestry Acts, 58 G. III., c. 69, and 59 G. III. c. 85; that is to say,—

If the aggregate amount of the assessment for the time being of any property belonging to such owner in such parish, or on any person or persons in respect of the same to the poor rate, shall not amount to 50l. .... } he will have 1 vote.

If the same shall amount to 50l. and not to 75l. .... } he will have 2 votes.

If the same shall amount to 75l. and not to 100l. .... } he will have 3 votes.

If the same shall amount to 100l. and not to 125l. .... } he will have 4 votes.

If the same shall amount to 125l. and not to 150l. .... } he will have 5 votes.

And if the same shall amount to 150l. or upwards .... } he will have 6 votes.

3. Any owner who shall be *bond fide* an occupier of any such property will be entitled to vote, as well in respect of his occupation as of his being such owner.

4. The Form marked A., hereto annexed, may be followed by owners of property, in making such statements of their claims to vote.

5. Any owner of such property may from time to time, by writing under his hand, appoint any person to vote as his proxy; but such proxy must, previous to the day of election, give to one of the churchwardens and overseers of such parish, a statement, in writing, of the name and address of his principal, and a description of the property in the parish or place, as proxy to the owner whereof he claims to vote; and also an original or attested copy of the writing, appointing him such proxy.

Regulations concerning the election qualifications of Guardians

The Guardians also rejoiced when one of their own members celebrated a special event, and such an occasion happened in August 1864 when Lord Lyttleton, Lord Lieutenant of the County reached his sixteenth year as Chairman of the Board of Guardians. He was presented with a testimonial in "the form of a portrait of the Dowager Lady Lyttleton, the noble Lord's mother and the commission for the execution of the work was entrusted to Mr. Weigel the well known painter." The presentation took place in the workhouse Board Room, and seventy guardians, past and present, attended the ceremony. Glowing tributes were

made of his hard work, leadership and dedication as chairman
- - - "the first to attend the meetings of the Guardians in the
Board Room and the last to leave." A full report on the
evening's proceedings duly appeared in the local press the
next day.

On the 15th June 1869 the Chairman was again feted
by the Guardians on his marriage. "This happy event took
place on the 10th inst, on which day all the inmates of the
workhouse were provided with a good dinner of roast beef
and plum pudding and a liberal supply of tobacco, snuff and
fruit cakes - - - the workhouse was gaily dressed with flowers,
wreaths and garlands and on the outside flags and banners
were displayed."

*Lord Lyttleton of Hagley Hall. Chairman of the Board
of Guardians in the 1860's.*

Later in the century another well known public figure became Chairman of the Guardians. John Amphlett was born in 1845 and spent his childhood at Churchill and Clent. He was educated at Bromsgrove School and at Worcester College, Oxford. He was called to the Bar of the Inner Temple in 1870. For many years he acted as Deputy Judge in the Worcester County Court District and also a Deputy Judge of the Birmingham County Court. He also served as a Magistrate of the Stourbridge Division.

He became the chairman of the Bromsgrove Board of Guardians where his legal knowledge was of great value. Mr. Holloway, the Clerk to the Union said of him "The genial manner of Mr. Amphlett made him a favourite with all and he will long be remembered for his services as Chairman of this Board for many years".

He travelled to the West Indies in 1872 to recover from a chest infection and on his return to England in 1873 he published the first of many books entitled "Under a Tropical Sky". The voyage stimulated his love of Natural History. In 1890 he published a "Short History of Clent" dedicated to Viscount Cobham of Hagley Hall. In 1908 he published the Genealogical history of his family under the title "Amphlett of Clent". He was also renowned locally for his many poems. As well as a classical scholar he was a keen geologist and made an intimate study of the Clent and Lickey Hills. He kept thirty-five folio volumes of his diaries from 1854 until his death in June 1918.

John Amphlett of Clent. Chairman of the Board of Guardians in the late 19th. century.

51

Some important figures from Bromsgrove and Redditch served as Guardians over the years. Three well known Redditch townspeople who served included Mr. Charles Bartleet, Edwin Smallwood (needle maker and co-founder of the Redditch Smallwood Hospital in 1895) and Mr. Samuel Allcock. The latter was a self made man and his wealth was based on fishing tackle manufacture, a trade which made Redditch famous throughout the western world. He was born in 1829, and built upon the fish hook trade already started by his father, Polycarp Allcock, in 1803. He encouraged skilled labour to migrate from Scotland, where the industry was already established, to Redditch to give expertise to the manufacture of fishing rods, reels, lines and salmon and trout flies. In 1866 Samuel published the first illustrated tackle catalogue, and in 1880 he boasted that his company was "the world's oldest and largest manufacturer of fishing tackle." His company expanded to the continent where three factories were set up; one in Spain and two in France. By the end of the nineteenth century his company was widely acknowledged as the world's largest fishing tackle manufacturer. Shortly after his death in the early twentieth century his Redditch company was employing one thousand workers, a considerable number in those days and the firm had gained over 30 gold medals and other high awards at leading International Exhibitions.

Samuel and his wife settled in a large mansion called the 'Cedars' in Redditch and the name of his wife appears on the Election for Guardians poster (see page 48). Samuel periodically accepted pauper boys from the workhouse to learn a trade as apprentices in his company.

The Board of Guardians prided themselves on their role within the Establishment. They always celebrated special state events and also mourned at an important bereavement. In May 1898 Mr. Gladstone, the Victorian giant of politics, died. The Board's minutes recorded "That the Board of Guardians and Rural District Council of Bromsgrove desire to express their respectful sympathy with the family and relatives of the late Mr. Gladstone and to add their testimony to the loss which the Nation has sustained." The family wrote back on the 15th June to thank the Board for their kind message of sympathy. Their greatest loss occurred in February 1901 with the death of Queen Victoria - - - - "The chairman moved that the Guardians of the Poor of the union of Bromsgrove desire to place on record their deep sense of the irreparable loss sustained by the British Empire and its Dependencies through the death of Her Most Gracious Majesty, Queen Victoria and to express their heartfelt sympathy with His Majesty King Edward VII and the rest of the Royal Family in their bereavement."

Samuel Allcock (third from the left). Famous Redditch fishing tackle manufacturer. Both he and his wife served as Guardians of the Bromsgrove Union workhouse

CHAPTER THREE

THE CARE OF PAUPER CHILDREN

1. Education
2. Apprenticeships
3. Emigration
4. Fostering

In the early years of the Union it was the duty of the Board to provide education for pauper children based in the workhouse. The first school teacher was appointed in February 1839. Miss Owen was only sixteen years old and received £10 p.a. for her duties. In June 1839 the Board received a complaint from the pauper children against Miss Owen and she was accused of being too severe in her attitude! The Board defended her against the charge and she retained her post.

In February 1848 a 'H.M. Inspector of Schools' visited the workhouse and amongst his recommendations appeared the following "that the master of the workhouse do occasionally employ the boys in the garden - - - - and that a blackboard and some maps should be procured." In July 1867, Mr. Bowyer, 'Inspector of Union Schools' visited the workhouse classroom and his report was barely satisfactory. "I have inspected the school and find the children as well instructed in scripture as usual. In reading, writing and arithmetic, however, many of them are not so forward as usual, which is accounted for by the fact of their being either more recently admitted or naturally dull." Most of the school teachers at the workhouse seem to have settled well and worked harmoniously. However one exception to the rule took place in the 1862-1863 period which involved the Mr. and Mrs. Pope crisis chapter which I have chronicled under another section. Mrs. Pope was the Matron of the Union, and she was well known for an abrasive tongue with both staff as well as inmates. Miss Dance, the then school teacher, fell foul of the matron in 1862. It ended unhappily for a trio of staff. She and Mr. and Mrs. Pope were asked for their resignations.

As the reader is aware state education in our country did not begin until the Forster Act of 1870. At last the mass of the working class was to be educated for the first time. Bravely the Church schools had tried to tackle the mounting problems of illiteracy until the government at last ended its 'laissez-faire' attitude and produced tax and rates to fund the new state system. The Guardians' attitude to the intervention of the state in education and to the question of funding these new Board schools out of local rates was vexed to say the least. The Board wanted to keep local rates down and realised that poor families in the surrounding Union might now come to the Guardians and ask for financial support, as parents still had to pay a small fee for the education of their children in the new 1870 Board schools. The frosty attitude is illustrated in this extract of the 24th June 1873 - - - "resolved to petition the House of Commons against the Elementary Education Act 1870 Amendment Bill which proposes to compel the Guardians to provide out of the Poor Rate for the education of all outdoor pauper children and also proposed that the school fees of the children of non-paupers who may satisfy the Guardians of their inability otherwise to comply with the compulsory bye-laws of a school Board, shall be paid by the Guardians out of the Rates - ordered that the petition be sent to Mr. R.P. Amphlett, M.P., and that he be requested to present it to the House of Commons." Little came of this appeal.

By the 21st September 1880 feelings were running high amongst the Guardians about this issue, so high that they decided to send a memorial to the Right Honourable Earl Spencer K.G., President of the "Lords of the Committee of Her Majesty's most honourable Privy Council on Education." The Bromsgrove Guardians also sent a copy of this to every Board of Guardians in England and Wales. The document included the following extacts:-

- - - - "that by the provisions of the Elementary Education Act 1870, 1873 and 1876 all children between the ages of 5 and 14 are required to attend school."

"That your memorialists fully admit the great benefits of a proper system of compulsory education is likely to confer upon the country at large, and the national importance of some of the legislative enactments which were introduced by the Elementary Education Act 1870, but they have nevertheless become fully convinced that the results of that legislation so far as it operates in requiring children to remain at school after the age of 12 years, prejudicially affect the industrial classes of the country, and is proving a source of serious inconvenience and loss to all connected with either agriculture or mercantile pursuits - - - - That it is all but impossible for a labouring man with a family to provide a bare subsistence for them by his own wages alone, and it appears nothing less than an injustice that he should be deprived of the wages which his children between 12 and 14 would be able to earn, if allowed to work."

"That to withdraw from the labour market, children between 12 and 14 years of age is injurious and prejudicial to manufacturers and agriculturalists in as much as their places must be filled by older persons at an advanced rate of wages causing serious loss of employees of labour in all branches of industry - - -. That in the opinion of your memorialists the burden of the ratepayers are considerable and unnecessarily increased by reason of such children being compelled to attend school, by the necessity for providing increased school accommodation by the payment of school fees, and the additional parochial relief which is thereby in many cases rendered necessary" - - - -.

Tension increased amongst the Guardians and in mid-July 1881 they clashed with the recently created Bromsgrove School Board. They complained against the resolution made by the Board - - - "that for the future all parents unable to pay the school fees of their children be referred to the Board of Guardians." The latter responded angrily - - - "it was unanimously resolved that the Clerk of the Union be directed to express the surprise of the Guardians that the School Board should by the resolution of the 5th May 1881 have presumed to refer all parents unable to pay the school fees of their children to the Board of Guardians - that the Guardians deny that the School Board have any such right, their power being limited either to remit fees, or refuse to do so - - - -.

"That looking to the fact that whether the school fees are remitted by the School Board, or paid by the Board of Guardians, the result will be the same - namely, payment by the ratepayers of the Parish of Bromsgrove. The Guardians think it strange that the School Board which were specially elected for educational purposes, should, by assuming to refer applicants to them (the Guardians) endeavour to evade their duties, and as a consequence to encourage applicants to mix and become familiar with the habits and applications of paupers who, unfortunately, are already too numerous." A battle royal then ensued between the Bromsgrove School Board and the Board of Guardians. Doubtless similar battles took place in other parts of England and Wales until the two systems dovetailed into each other as they have fully done so by today.

Good sense prevailed, and on the 18th October 1881 we read in the minute book that the Guardians themselves had decided to send workhouse children to the Board school. "It is proposed that this Board do not advertise for a schoolmistress for the Union workhouse, but that all children therein of school age be sent to the Stourbridge Road Board School, Bromsgrove, but if there should not be sufficient room there, that the elder children be sent to the Lickey End Board School." The Guardians decided as a result of this decision to close the workhouse school room which had been in use since February 1839. Why did the Guardians have a change of heart? Did they realise that at least some small saving could be made now that the services of the workhouse teacher could be dispensed with? Twenty children were sent to Stourbridge Road schools and the remainder were sent to Lickey End schools, and their fees were paid quarterly.

In November 1881 measles and scarlet fever broke out in the workhouse and affected the children badly and Dr. Carey ruled that they should not be allowed to go to their schools until the illnesses had cleared. In March 1883 the Guardians were reprimanded by a Local Government Board Inspector who made pointed references to the "overcrowded conditions of some of the sick wards and the want of separate wards for sick women and children" and also to "the want of some extra garments for children going to school in wet weather - - -. In reference to the sick book it will be noticed that many children have of late suffered from colds and bronchitis caused by retaining wet clothes in school - this need has not been supplied and consequently the children have frequently to be kept away from school for whole days." The Board of Guardians subsequently agreed to capes being purchased for the pauper children to wear for school.

The question of health of pauper school children concerned not just the Local Government Board, but also the local school authority as illustrated by this letter addressed to the Clerk of the Union.

Lickey End Board School,
Bromsgrove. October 5th 1885

Dear Sir,

I don't know whether the attendance of the Union children is in any way under your control, but if so, it is high time something was done. Only one week out of the last five have they attended regularly and now they are absent again this afternoon. This is most annoying as such fluctuations and uncertain attendance has such damaging effect upon the average and upon the government grant which is paid upon the average.

"Only three children in the whole school are absent this afternoon besides this batch, and yet the average attendance for the week is ruined!

I am sorry to complain but I think silence would be neglecting the interests of the Board."

Yours truly,
William Thorneycroft
(headteacher)

Whether this letter was the straw which broke the camel's back is debatable, but significantly within weeks of its receipt the Guardians were advertising for a schoolmistress for the workhouse children at £25 p.a. No-one applied for the post and it was re-advertised. Only two applied for it and a Mrs. Tyers of Hightown near Liverpool was appointed. The Local Government Board displayed a measure of disapproval with the decision of the Guardians "to discontinue sending the children, inmates of the workhouse to Public Elementary Schools" and refused to approve the appointment of the new mistress until they were satisfied that the Board had bought the necessary educational material. Whatever the reasons, there was a very high turnover of school mistresses in the next few years and this must have unsettled the children to some extent. The stubborn Guardians were quite determined not to send its children to the public elementary school and in May 1890 the Board issued clear duties to the school mistress clearly shunning the prospect of integration and emphasising its independance from the public sector of education. Some of these well defined duties included:-

1. "To instruct the boys and girls who are inmates of the workhouse for three of the working hours at least every day in Reading, Writing and Arithmetic and the principles of the Christian religion and such other instruction shall be imparted to them as may fit them for service and train the habits of usefulness, industry and virtue."

2. "To regulate the discipline and arrangements of the school and the industrial and moral training of the children subject to the direction of the Guardians and to superintend the children out of school hours as well as during the periods when they are actually under instruction."

3. "To accompany the children when they quit the workhouse for exercise or for attendance at public worship

unless the Guardians shall otherwise direct."

4. "To keep the children clean in their persons and orderly and decorous in their conduct."

5. "To assist the master and matron respectively in maintaining due subordination in the workhouse."

However, within two years the wounds between the School Board and Board of Guardians had sufficiently healed to prompt the latter to start sending children to the Lickey End Board School as from February 1892. Suitable clothing was bought for the children; those aged four to six years were given suits costing 5s/6d, and those aged seven years to sixteen years were given suits costing 10s/11d.

What happened to the workhouse teacher? She was given a testimonial on the 1st March 1892 - - - "The Board have pleasure in stating that Miss Mary Simons has held the post of schoolmistress at this workhouse for about seven years and that the children in the month of February 1892 being sent to the Board School for their education she was appointed as Assistant Matron of the workhouse. That during the whole period of her service she has given entire satisfaction to the Board in the discharge of her duties - carried unanimously." This action ranks surely as one of the earliest examples of re-deployment in the teaching profession!

Lickey End Board School (now Lickey End First School)
Thomas Carter a pauper boy from the Bromsgrove
Workhouse was made to suffer excessive corporal punishment
here in May 1898

The relationship between Guardians and School Board continued on an even keel until an incident in 1898 threatened its stability once again. On the 3rd May a pauper boy named Thomas Carter who was boarded out with James Perrygrove of Lickey End, was brought before the Board by Perrygrove Senior who stated "that about a week previously the boy was struck by a teacher named Mrs. Drewitt at the Lickey End Board School across the top of his nose and eye causing bad bruises and also that he was caned on the legs causing weals. The man stated further that a great deal of cruelty took place at these schools and the children were constantly being hit. He admitted that Mrs. Drewitt had said the cut across the boy's face was accidentally done." Corporal punishment was quite acceptable in schools of the Victorian period and the cane was regularly used; but this incident seemed harsh even by Victorian standards. The Guardians were displeased with the treatment received by the boy and set up a committee to look into the facts. On the 14th June 1898 a letter was received from the Clerks of the Bromsgrove School Board transmitting a copy of the report made by the committee appointed to enquire into the complaint. It ended with the words - - - "the stroke of the cane in the face was purely accidental and the result of it trivial." That seems to have been the end of the matter. There is no further reference in the minute books to the incident! The whole episode seems to have been hushed up.

The prime aim of apprenticeships for pauper children was to lessen the financial burden on the Union. However, the Board was careful in its choice of occupations and was anxious to safeguard the future welfare of its young charges.

The first stage in setting up an apprenticeship was done when the Guardians advertised the fact that there were youngsters in the workhouse who were old enough to work. These advertisements were placed in local newspapers and interested employers then contacted the Board. The potential employer was then interviewed by the Guardians as to his suitability, and if the Board agreed, the youngster was released into the care of his new master for a month's trial. At the end of the four weeks a decision was then taken by both parties including the young person. The latter was then apprenticed for a term of between four and six years. Indentures in duplicate were then signed and sealed when the youngster accepted these terms.

In the early years of the Union many boys were sent to the mining and metal-based trades of the 'Black Country' and advertisements were regularly placed in Stourbridge and Brierley Hill newspapers. In January 1838 three boys were sent to Darlaston. In June 1847 a Richard Band left the workhouse with the intention of becoming a miner, but had to return to the Union because of weak eyesight. In 1848 many youngsters were sent to the iron and coal industries. In October 1850 two 13 year old boys were apprenticed to Abel Carter of Wednesbury, a gun lock maker. The boys were given two suits of clothing each and taken to Birmingham where their employer collected them. In December 1850 two boys were apprenticed to Thomas Millington, a miner of Wednesbury. Not all the 'Black Country' jobs on offer were in heavy industry. In January 1867 a Mr. Joseph Bird of Birmingham, engraver, applied to have Solomon Reeves aged eleven as an apprentice. In September 1853 a youth was apprenticed to a Dudley bricklayer, and in September 1864 a George Waterson was given a month's trial with Mr. James Wooley of Dudley, a basket maker. In May 1873 George Guest aged 13 was apprenticed to a stirrup iron maker at Walsall. One of the most unusual apprenticeships on record also took place in the 'Black Country' in August 1841 - - - "ordered that measures be taken for binding Nicholas Tilt as an apprentice to John Brucknell of Dudley, a hairdresser, and that a two pound premium be given with him in consequence of his being a weakly boy and not fit for laborious occupation."

From the 1850's more pauper children were employed in the immediate neighbourhood and especially in the expanding needle and fish hook trades of the growing town of Redditch. In June 1856 the son of Widow Hawkes was placed with Mr. Buffins of Beoley Needle Mills, in Redditch, on trial preparatory to his being apprenticed. In July 1869 Mr. Dennis Robinson, a fish hook maker of Redditch applied to have Charles Taylor, one of the boys in the workhouse as an apprentice to learn his trade. One month later in August, having completed the month's trial we read "resolved that the boy be bound to the said Dennis Robinson for six years to learn his trade of fish hook maker and that he be required to pay the boy six pence per week for the fourth and fifth years of the term and one shilling per week for the last year, and that a premium of two suits of clothing be now provided for the said boy." Indentures in duplicate were then signed and sealed. A similar contract was signed in 1871 when Joseph Depper aged 15 was accepted for a six year apprenticeship by the well known Redditch fish hook maker and fishing tackle manufacturer, Samuel Allcock. The employer who also served as a Guardian for a short time, agreed to pay the boy "three pence weekly wages during the first two years, six pence weekly during the third and fourth years, and one shilling weekly during the fifth and sixth years." There are a number of other apprenticeship examples in the Redditch metal based trades in the same period. Very few pauper girls were apprenticed from the workhouse. One of the rare ones occurred in May 1873 when a Mr. George Scriven of Redditch, painter and glazier, applied to have Sarah Ann Warman aged twelve into his service.

Not all the apprenticeships survived the test of time, and a number of indentures were broken for a variety of reasons. In December 1866 the Board received a letter from William Brown, a chain maker from Quarry Bank, Brierley Hill, to say that his apprentice, Thomas Parkes had absconded. Mr. Dennis Robinson of Redditch, mentioned earlier in this section, was also dissatisfied with the boy Charles Taylor by October 1871 after just two years - - - "he applied to have the indenture cancelled on the grounds of the boy's misbehaviour, and of his been convicted and imprisoned for stealing fruit." In May 1873 James Smith complained against his master Mr. Joseph Mogg, also a Guardian. He complained of ill treatment and claimed that he was not being taught a trade. The two were summoned before the Board to ascertain the true facts and as a result of the interview the boy was reprimanded for obstinacy and Mr. Mogg was thanked for disciplining the boy. In February 1886 a local lady farmer from Belbroughton complained against Thomas Amiss who had been in her service for ten months. She claimed that the boy had killed some of her poultry and a goose and he had also run away. Thomas countered by saying that his mistress was cruel and that he had to work without shoes, or was given shoes that were too small for him. In July 1886 a William Henry Crocket, who had completed five years of his apprenticeship to Edward Monks, a Redditch file cutter was summoned before the Board on a charge of having spoiled some files, and that the charge, if further pressed by his employer, might end up at the Redditch Petty Sessions. In July 1892 we read in the minutes of another failure - - - "Mrs. Bates' letter of Smallheath, Birmingham was read out stating that the girl, Catherine Fisher will not do as she is told and that she cannot keep her any longer. It was ordered that the girl be returned to the workhouse."

Obviously some of the pauper children were most unhappy in their new situations and remind us of the trials and tribulations of Oliver Twist. It was not until June 1873 that the Local Government Board decided to act in such instances. Relieving Officers were then asked to check up on the working conditions of all young pauper apprentices under the age of sixteen years. Maybe as a response to this new ruling a request received on the 11th June 1873 from Mr. Samuel Coley, Walsall iron founder to have two boys as apprentices was turned down by the Guardians because the work was regarded as too heavy and dangerous for two young boys.

There are many examples of pauper apprentices settling happily in their new positions. In June 1873 the minutes record "Mr. Joseph Davenport of Quinton attended with Ellen Ince (who had been with his family as a domestic servant on their farm for a month's trial) and the child having expressed a wish to remain with Mr. Davenport where she had been kindly treated - - - it was ordered that the child be allowed to return to the service of Mrs. Davenport she having stated that the child would only be required to discharge very little duties as a domestic servant and undertaking to teach her to read and write and to provide her with clothing - ordered that two suits of clothes be allowed to the child." In a few months Mr. and Mrs. Davenport asked for another pauper inmate to join Ellen Ince at their farm, and a boy named Samuel Taylor aged eleven was sent.

Another pleasing apprenticeship took place in March 1897. Frederick Broadley a pauper boy of the workhouse was allowed to join the 'International Steam Trawling Company', Grimsby under the usual conditions of apprenticeship. A letter was received a couple of weeks later from the company stating that the lad was off on a fishing expedition to Iceland. On May 4th the Board received a letter from Frederick "stating that he liked the sea and would rather be on the sea than on land and that after another trip he should be bound." The boy soon signed the indentures as an apprentice and the Board received at least two letters from him in the next few months stating how happy he was in his occupation.

Another successful training appears in the minute book in December 1897. A letter was received from the Secretary of the Blind Institution, Edgbaston, Birmingham stating that the youth James Jones "had made very satisfactory progress with his basket making trade and would eventually make an efficient worker." The Board was well pleased with the report and decided to continue with the payments for his upkeep until his training was complete.

The Board considered it a moral duty to find employment for paupers, and hoped that work would make them willing employees and therefore independent of the Union's finances. However, in certain periods of the nineteenth century work was almost impossible to find and this caused severe hardships, e.g. the 1840's were known as the 'Hungry Forties'. The Board adopted another measure to counter the effects of such unemployment and social misery, and this policy was that of encouraging emigration. Waves of emigrants left Britain for a new life at well defined periods in the Victorian era. Poverty was one of the major causes, and the lure of a new life and a new beginning resulted in millions leaving Britain. In the years 1861 to 1890 one and a half million people emigrated from Britain to the USA. Almost 350,000 went to Canada; a further 500,000 moved to Australia. A total of 4.6 million emigrated to the USA in the 1851-1920 period. In all well over 11 million emigrated from Britain to the above countries in the 1851-1920 period.

Like many other Unions, the Bromsgrove Union also participated in the emigration process. Emigration offered a release for many paupers that would otherwise drain the finances of the workhouse union. In the early years, however, the local Union was hesitant in helping potential emigrants simply because it claimed it was unable to fund these passages to the new world.

Paupers who wished to leave these shores were often unable to meet the costs of the sea journey and had to ask the Union for financial support. In March 1850 the Board turned down the request of William Hall, his wife and six children for financial support to help them emigrate to the Cape of Good Hope, South Africa. The Board felt unable to meet the seven pound a head passage fare. In 1852 many local people wished to leave the Bromsgrove area and to emigrate to Commonwealth countries, or to countries of the Empire as they were known then. They sent their names to the Emigration Office in London, and in July 1852 the Guardians were sanctioned by the Poor Law Commission to pay the passage of five families. Another dimension appeared in May 1873 when a letter was received by the Board from a Miss Rye who wanted to know "whether there were any little girls in the workhouse she could have to take out to her home in Canada with a view of placing them in good situations." It transpired that Miss Rye was an agent of the Canadian Immigration Department and her brief was to encourage migration to that growing nation. The Guardians considered her letter and on the 24th June 1873 responded "It was resolved that the several poor children residing in the workhouse, being desirous of emigrating to Canada, the necessary steps be immediately taken to effect the emigration and that a sum not exceeding £13 be expended for each child and be charged upon the common fund." The Board then drew up the list of nine small girls from the workhouse who would be handed over to Miss Rye.

Eliza Lyddall	orphan	aged 7 years
Sarah Warman	deserted	aged 12 years
Jane Warman	deserted	aged 5 years

Sarah and Jane Warman were sisters.

Mary Young	deserted	aged 6 years
Louisa Burke	orphan	aged 10 years
Emma Taylor	orphan	aged 10 years
Susan Price	deserted	aged 10 years
Sarah Matthews	orphan	aged 10 years
Ellen Matthews	orphan	aged 5 years

Sarah and Ellen were sisters.

Was the Board correct to take this decision? Did the youngsters know where Canada was and how far it was from England? Did the Board decide to send these girls to a strange land in order to save money in the long term for the Union, or did the Board believe that Canada offered a better life for them than the West Midlands? Whatever the answers, news of the proposed emigration seeped out into the town of Bromsgrove and caused much gossip and also heartache. The mother of Mary Young who had deserted her as a baby turned up at the workhouse. Having declared her identity she pleaded with the Board not to send her daughter to Canada, and claimed that her brother, Mr. Henry Young, a seaman residing at Southsea was prepared to foster Mary. A letter was duly received from Mr. Young endorsing his sister's wish. The stubborn Guardians were reticent to consider this application at such a delicate stage in the emigration procedure but thankfully they were overruled by the Local Government Board which stated that Mary Young could not emigrate to Canada without her mother's consent. The story, therefore, had a happy ending and little Mary's name was removed from the list and she was allowed to leave the workhouse and travel to her uncle's home in Southsea. In contrast to this episode, a few weeks later in August 1873 an odd request was received from a Harriet Depper, a single woman and inmate of the workhouse who "was desirous of her illegitimate child aged 6 years, also an inmate of the workhouse, being allowed to emigrate to Canada." The mother did not stipulate that she wanted to accompany her daughter. Why did Harriet request such a thing? Did she not realise that she would never see her daughter again or did she realise this but hoped that this sacrifice would secure her daughter a better life in a new country? Whatever her reasoning, her decision surely was a heartbreaking one. The Guardians agreed immediately to her request and the name of little Elizabeth Depper was added to the small party.   The nine girls were then taken by the workhouse master and school mistress to meet Miss Rye at Princes Landing Stage, Liverpool on Wednesday, 17th September 1873.   The ship sailed the same day and took the small group away from these shores.   Late in December 1873 a letter was received from Miss Rye to say that the nine girls had settled well; that five had been adopted and the other four had been apprenticed to respectable persons.   Miss Rye wrote again in April 1874 offering to take more children to Canada in May 1874; this time she wanted ten orphaned or deserted boys as well as ten orphaned or deserted girls.   For reasons unknown the Guardians agreed to the emigration of only four girls: Laura and Jane Banner who were orphaned sisters aged 11 years and 9 years respectively, and Eliza Bird and Jane Bird aged 9 years and 6 years who were proposed by their father who was a workhouse pauper.   Was this yet another noble yet heartbreaking sacrifice by a pauper parent?   The party of four again met Miss Rye at Liverpool and embarked for Canada.

'Here and There'.   Many local paupers emigrated in the 1840's.

In July 1874 the Guardians received a letter from the Local Government Board informing them of its decision "to instruct one of their inspectors to visit Canada with a view of ascertaining generally the present condition of the children who had already emigrated." Whatever the outcome of this visit the Bromsgrove Workhouse Union did not send any more pauper children to Canada within the period coverd by this publication. However, the Union did receive several requests from local pauper families at this time for help in paying their passage to Canada. One of these was a Sarah Jones, a widow aged 28 years who wanted to take her five children ranging from 6 years to 7 weeks with her to Canada to join her father. Sarah Jones said that her father would pay the passage costs, but could the Board help with clothing and arrange transport to the port of Liverpool? The Guardians agreed to the request, realising that in the long term the finances of the Union would benefit if a party of six paupers were to leave the area!

Accounts for the half-year ending in October 1874 reveals that emigration subsidies from the Bromsgrove Union totalled £64-11s-3d, quite a large sum in those days. The year 1873-1874 must therefore have been a year of despair and agonising decision making for many local paupers.

After an interval of sixteen years a letter was received from Miss Rye in May 1890. Doubtless that Miss Rye had been collecting many pauper children from other workhouse unions in the meantime, and her new letter contained the old request - - - - "a letter was received enquiring if this Board would care to send any of their Protestant girls between the ages of 9 and 13 with her to Canada in August 1890. Ordered that Miss Rye be informed that there are not any children in the workhouse eligible." A second letter was received from the persistent Miss Rye but once again the Guardians gave a negative response. Why the change of attitude? Was the Board telling the truth? The workhouse did house pauper children in 1890, but the policy towards emigration at this time had changed. Instead, the Bromsgrove Union was allowing pauper children to go to foster homes in the locality. The last entry on emigration within the period covered by this book appears on the 10th January 1899 when a communication was received from the Secretary of 'Dr. Barnado's Homes for Orphan Waifs' stating that they were prepared to act as agents for sending out children to Canada.

The Board's policy seems to have changed from encouraging the emigration of pauper children to sending them to foster parents in the local area; for one thing it was much cheaper! This system was introduced in the early 1880's. Foster parents were initially given some small allowance to help in the upkeep of the children. The idea was adopted also because it socially integrated the pauper children with their peers and with adults and broke down the stigmatic barrier between pauperism and society. The fostered children were periodically visited by members of the Board. Most of the children seem to have settled down extremely well with their new parents. In April 1887 the Guardians said of John Reading who had settled in an Alvechurch home that "he was turning out admirably and he was much beloved by his foster mother." A similar comment applied to Fanny Amiss who had settled "well and has a comfortable home" in Stoke Heath.

In October 1890 one foster child was adopted by her new mother "Mrs. James attended and asked to be allowed to take Minnie Whitehouse from the workhouse and adopt her as her own child. Resolved unanimously that the application be granted."

Some of the children indeed were adopted and others remained with their foster parents until the age of sixteen as seen in this extract of October 1892 - - - "that the child Charlotte Eaton aged 4 be boarded out with Miss Lacey on the usual terms. Also that the child shall be under the control of the Guardians until she reaches the age of sixteen years."

Sadly some children did not settle in their new homes as was the case in November 1892 - - - "The Board considered the case of James Monk, a boarded-out case returned to the workhouse by the foster mother on account of his bad conduct and his stealing and cashing a postal order. It was resolved that the child remain in the workhouse pending inquiries being made with a view to getting him into an industrial school." In December 1892 he was sent to Hereford Industrial School. The story of James Monk, however, turned out happily in the end. We read in July 1896 that having completed his training he was able to find employment with Messrs. Henderson & Spalding, Printers, London and was in receipt of a good wage "and that he will be carefully looked after for at least the next three years."

In February 1896 three children were given to foster parents. In May 1896 a letter was received from Charlotte Briggs asking that her sister now boarded out with a lady at Clent might be allowed into her custody. The Guardians decided that the child should remain with her foster mother for at least another six weeks. On the 9th June 1896 a letter was received from a Robert Wilson of Glasgow who was the uncle of the fostered child asking the Board to release her to his care. The Board again faltered "the girl had better remain where she is and that they (the Guardians) had no means of paying her railway fare to Glasgow." Within two weeks the Board allowed the girl to depart for Scotland on hearing that her family had sent the money to pay the child's railway fare!

CHAPTER FOUR

THE WORKHOUSE SPIRIT

1. Thrift in action.
2. Troublesome paupers and punishments.
3. A more caring attitude:
   (a) Visiting Committees
   (b) Care of the mentally ill
   (c) Compassion

There are many examples in the minute book of the attitudes of the Guardians towards saving money within its area. Some of their thrifty methods seem unsavoury compared to the benefits we enjoy today within the framework of the welfare state. All parishes within the Union were responsible for collecting their own poor rates, and looking after their own paupers whether at home (outrelief) or contributing towards their upkeep within the workhouse (in-relief). Some of the smaller parishes were constantly in debt to the Union. In December 1837 Belbroughton fell into arrears, but the Union was unsympathetic and exerted pressure on the parish to pay its dues. Belbroughton offered to sell its old workhouse building to raise the necessary funds, but its offer was turned down by the Union. At the same time the parish of Stoke Prior fell into debt. The timing of both crises is obviously linked to the weather - a bad winter, and the able bodied were unable to work out of doors, which forced them to turn to the parish for relief. The worse the weather the more paupers applied for relief and the greater the financial strain on the small parish. It is clearly seen in the minute books that weather and the seasons were all important in the cyclic pattern of employment and social distress. In January 1838 many appeals were heard by the Union from people who felt unable to pay the poor rates at that period, asking to be excused payment until the next quarter, but most of these appeals were rejected by the Board of Guardians.

In one week in January 1838 a total of £46-7s-3d was

spent on outdoor relief, which was an extremely high figure (£31-8s-1d was given in money and £14-19s-2½d in kind. Three hundred and thirty four loaves of bread were distributed.) The numbers of indoor paupers also increased during the month, and on the 15th January 1838 the Board made a ruling that "no paupers be admitted into the workhouse after 12.00 o'clock on Saturdays." In the summer of 1838 the Board tried to recoup some of its losses and brought pressure on some paupers on out relief. On the 16th July the minutes read "Resolved that the outdoor relief list for the parish of Bromsgrove (the largest parish in the Union) be revised and that the paupers chargeable to the parish be required to attend at the Board room on Monday 30th July and the two following Mondays after the business of the day to show cause why the relief should be continued." In July there were 55 paupers in Bromsgrove on outdoor relief, and twenty two in the parish of Tardebigge. Before the end of the year however, the Union was well pleased with the money it had saved within its area since its founding, a saving of some 25% - - - - "such saving not being effected by diminishing the comforts of the aged, infirm or really destitute, but in the better check which the present system affords to the imposition of the idle and worthless."

One of the worst examples of the Boards inhumanity towards the able bodied seeking relief came in the first three months of 1848, a year well known for its bad weather and also political upheavals in western and central Europe. The local unemployed in this period included nailers and agricultural labourers who found themselves temporarily out of work. The Guardians became increasingly worried by the escalating costs and the numbers swelling into the workhouse; some 324 paupers by the end of February 1848. The able bodied in the workhouse received harsh words from the Board and told to break stones in the yard (at least half-a-yard a day). Failure to do this would result in an appearance before the local magistrate and a probable jail sentence. This ultimatum seems to have only hardened the resolve of the able bodied paupers, and five of them were committed to prison for 21 days hard labour each. In early March the workhouse was overflowing with paupers and the Board ordered the removal of all single able bodied male paupers from the workhouse in order to relieve the congestion. They were promised outdoor relief in cash and kind provided they performed stone breaking in the community. The result was a mutiny - all such paupers refused to leave the workhouse! Seven of the ringleaders were taken before the JP who committed each of them to prison for 21 days with hard labour.

FORM 9.—The Pauper Description Book.

UNION. Parish of _____

1 No. in Application List or Admission and Discharge Book.	2 Names of Paupers, their Wives, and Children under 16, dependent on them.	3 Year when Born.	4 Residence, where, and with whom.	5 Calling.	6 If Adult, whether Single, Married, Widow, or Widower: if Child, whether Orphan, Deserted or Bastard.	7 If able-bodied.	8 If partially or wholly Disabled, description of the Disability.	9 Present cause of seeking Relief, and if receiving any assistance from Clubs, Charitable Institution, Government Pensions, or other sources.	10 Date when first chargeable.	10 Names, &c. of Relations liable under 43d Eliz.,—Distinguishing those apparently able to assist the Pauper, their earnings, and other means (if any).	11 OBSERVATIONS. Death, Removals, and such other Information as may be deemed useful.

The figures at the head of the columns correspond with those in the Application and Report Book (Schedule D., Form 21), and in the Admission and Discharge Book (Schedule C., Form 15).

FORM 10.—Abstract of the Application and Report Book, with Board's decisions on Applications, for the Quarter ending _____

Parish of _____

_____ Union.

No. in Relief List.	Name of Applicant.	Age.	Particulars and Number of Family.	Relief given, if any, at the discretion of Relieving Officer.		Relief ordered by Guardians.				For what time allowed, or nature of the Order made.	Week when allowed.	Initials of Presiding Guardian.
				Value in Kind.	Week when given.	Money.	Kind. Quantity & Description.		Value.			
				s. d.		s. d.			s. d.			

Form 9. The Pauper Description Book

WEEKLY OUT-DOOR RELIEF LIST, for the Quarter ending 183 ,

Parish of   District.   *Relieving Officer.*

Number in Application Book	Males	Females	Adults	Children under 16.	The gross Number of Children under 16 re-lieved with Parents.	Name of the Pauper, and Wife, if any.	When Born.	If not residing in Parish, where resident.	No. of the Class in the Quarterly Abstract.	For what Period Relief ordered.	Week when ordered.	1st Week.		2d Week.		3d Week.		4th Week.		5th Week.		6th Week.		7th Week.		8th Week.		9th Week.		10th Week.		11th Week.		12th Week.		13th Week.		Total in Money and in Kind.
												In Money.	In Kind.	In Money.	In Kind.	In Money.	In Kind.	In Money.	In Kind.	In Money.	In Kind.	In Money.	In Kind.	In Money.	In Kind.	In Money.	In Kind.	In Money.	In Kind.	In Money.	In Kind.	In Money.	In Kind.	In Money.	In Kind.	In Money.	In Kind.	£. *s.* *d.*
												s. d.	*s. d.*	*s. d.*	*s. d.*	*s. d.*	*s. d.*	*s. d.*	*s. d.*	*s. d.*	*s. d.*	*s. d.*	*s. d.*	*s. d.*	*s. d.*	*s. d.*	*s. d.*	*s. d.*	*s. d.*	*s. d.*	*s. d.*	*s. d.*	*s. d.*	*s. d.*	*s. d.*	*s. d.*	*s. d.*	
TOTALS						Total in Money and Value in Kind each Week. *Note.*—The numbers in the first three columns are to follow consecutively, and *then* to be prefixed to the name in the "Application Book."						£. *s. d.*	*s. d.*	£. *s. d.*	*s. d.*	£. *s. d.*	*s. d.*	£. *s. d.*	*s. d.*	£. *s. d.*	*s. d.*	£. *s. d.*	*s. d.*	£. *s. d.*	*s. d.*	£. *s. d.*	*s. d.*	£. *s. d.*	*s. d.*	£. *s. d.*	*s. d.*	£. *s. d.*	*s. d.*	£. *s. d.*	*s. d.*	£. *s. d.*	*s. d.*	£. *s. d.*

Form 25a. *Weekly Out-door Relief List*

Vagrancy was also on the increase in 1848, and by November the situation was very worrying for the Guardians. On the 27th November they ordered the Chief Constable to crack down on the many troublesome vagrants in Bromsgrove with a view to dispersing them. The Union was expected to provide for vagrants, and if they could be dispersed and scattered then there would be fewer claims. The crackdown did take place, but the hardy types still remained and the arrest then took place of a few ringleaders including a female vagrant by the name of Maria Jones, who had maliciously broken several panes of glass at the tramp house or shelter in the town. She was tried and given a stiff prison sentence.

In July 1865 sixteen police officers were appointed to serve as inspectors of nuisances in the Bromsgrove Union districts. Their main role in this capacity was to check on the comings and goings of the many tramps or vagrants. The Guardians had a duty to give relief to this class of pauper, but had always complained about the high cost of relief, the bad behaviour of certain tramps, and the escalating costs in maintaining the two tramp houses or doss houses in Bromsgrove and Redditch. In January 1867 the weather pushed up the costs yet again, and the Guardians acted swiftly to solve the problem. The two doss houses were done away with and a ticket system was applied to all vagrants. In future incoming vagrants were expected to fill in tickets indicating where they had come from and where they were heading. Those tramps who could prove that they were able bodied poor in search of work were given a bed and food for one night only, in the workhouse building. The other condition was that they should have travelled at least 20 miles that day in search of employment. Such claimants were placed in the vagrant ward in the workhouse and "be supplied with four ounces of bread on their arrival, allowed to sleep there and be supplied with four ounces of bread the next morning, and if his behaviour has been good, the master will sign that he has complied with the regulations and allow him to depart in the morning without exacting any work - - - the sleeping accommodation in the vagrant wards shall consist of a platform constructed of inclined boards with a sufficiency of straw, and rugs in severe weather."

Tramps who were discovered loitering within the local area, and not looking for work were to be placed in the workhouse and given many unpleasant tasks such as oakum picking, bone and stone smashing etc. A guilty "male vagrant will have to break a quarter of a yard of stones, or pick one pound of oakum, and if a female have to pick half a pound of oakum either on that day or the next morning."

Similar 'work' had to be done by all able bodied indoor paupers by March 1867.

The new ticket system worked to the satisfaction of the Board as the half-year comment states - - - - "there was a decrease of 607 in the number of vagrants relieved and a saving of £34-3s-1d." The master's extra workload in tending to the vagrants was acknowledged and his salary was increased from £50 p.a. to £60 p.a. After twelve months the Guardians discovered that there was a decrease in relief of 1650 vagrants. The Guardians were well pleased in the cost cutting exercise, but hopefully the reader realises that the problem of vagrancy and pauperism had simply been diverted elsewhere, or "brushed under the carpet." The thoughtless Board's brief was to save money and deter people from applying for relief, not to solve the problem of pauperism. One should also realise that most of the vagrants were able bodied persons searching for work, but the Board's attitude was to feed and bed them for one night and then show them the door the next morning with instructions to walk at least 20 miles before evening looking for work.

The year 1867 was a bad year for the finances of the workhouse as illustrated by these vagrancy measures. In June 1867 the Guardians took another unpopular step in saving money - - - "that the master be present at the opening of all letters by inmates of the workhouse, and in case any letter to any inmate shall contain any money or stamps the master is hereby authorised to take possession thereof from each inmate, and to appropriate the same in repayment of his or her relief - - - - carried unanimously."

'The Law of Settlement' element in the New Poor Law Act of 1834 only enhanced the 'Scrooge' image of the workhouses. Unions were encouraged to move paupers from their area to workhouses in the parishes of their births, and this created serious hardships and heartbreak. Unions were sometimes drawn into conflict as they refused to accept paupers from other Unions, and frequent proceedings were held in a court of law to settle the matter.

Migrant Irish paupers were universally disliked by the Unions, and there are a few examples of the anti-Irish feelings in the operating of the Bromsgrove Union, with frequent attempts at deportation. The case of the Irish father and daughter appeared on the 6th August 1838 "ordered that measures be taken for the removal of John Morrison and his daughter Mary Morrison to Ireland, they having become chargeable to Bromsgrove parish and never having done any act to gain settlement in this county."

Poor John Morrison, however, was not deported. Did

he feign insanity in order to stay at the workhouse? This is a question I cannot answer, but the ruling against him dictated a far worse fate than deportation or workhouse - - - - 3rd September 1838 "The clerk reported that John Morrison supposed to have been born in Ireland was still in the Bromsgrove workhouse, and that overseers of Bromsgrove were not in a situation to prove that he has any legal place of settlement and that he is insane. Ordered that means be taken to remove him to the Droitwich Lunatic Asylum, and that the cost of his maintenance be paid by the county out of county rates!"

Another anti-Irish example appeared in June 1847, and this clearly illustrates the prejudice of the Board. "The relieving officer and guardian for Redditch reported that much difficulty had been experienced lately by the assistant overseer in administrating relief to Irish vagrants." He had been unable to find accommodation for them in the town, and a few weeks later the assistant overseer of Redditch reported that "he could not succeed in procuring any premises for the occupation of the Irish vagrants in consequence of fever and other objections to which that class are subject!"

In January 1850 the Board's anger was clearly evident in the minute book after their failure to deport an Irish family from Redditch via Liverpool to Belfast.

The anti-Irish feeling again appears in 1851, and once more in the town of Redditch when in April of that year the Board received a petition from a few Redditch townspeople against four Irish families sharing a house in the town. The complaint focused on the generally "filthy condition of the house" and also against "the large number of rabbits also housed there."

There are many examples of the Board moving paupers against their will from the local area to the parish of their births within the West Midlands. On the 8th January 1838 a letter was signed by the chairman of the Union and sent to Mr. Holyoake, overseer of Tardebigge, requesting him "to take immediate measures to remove Harriet, John and George Hill to Solihull, the Yarnold family to their parish - - - and to ascertain whether the late husband of widow White did not belong to Feckenham." On the 27th July 1853 the following entry appeared "Charlotte, the wife of Thomas Finch resident of Belbroughton being reported insane and her place of settlement appearing to be Inkberrow. Ordered that the Alcester Board of Guardians be requested to pay expenses of conveying the lunatic to the County Asylum and for her maintenance there, without an order of the Justices."

In July 1865 yet another example of the 'Law of Settlement' - "The clerk reported that in the case of William Steele, lunatic, he had discovered his place of settlement to be the parish of Birmingham and that the requisite steps will be taken with a view of getting back the expenses incurred on his account, £9-1s-6d." At first the Birmingham workhouse denied all responsibility, but after the Bromsgrove Union's decision to call in the Justices to rule the case, Birmingham reluctantly accepted to foot the bill.

On the 6th November 1866 a similar story unfolded when Thomas Prosser and his three children were moved to the reluctant Pershore workhouse. There are also many examples of the Board contesting the inward flow of paupers from other parishes. In November 1838 the Union appealed successfully against the Bradford Union who wished to send a William Richardson and his family to Bromsgrove. In October 1847 the following entry "Ordered that the clerk write to the Droitwich Board of Guardians and request to be informed under what circumstances the Bailey family were discharged from the workhouse of that Union they having become chargeable to this Union through illness under which they laboured at Droitwich."

Examples of goodwill and co-operation between workhouses were rare, but a solitary example appeared in May 1853 when a request from the Alcester Board of Guardians for a few of the Bromsgrove Union workhouse paupers to visit Alcester was granted. The purpose of the visit was to show the Alcester paupers how to produce mats, which were then sold and the money used in the general maintenance of the workhouse paupers.

The Board did accept its responsibility towards paupers born within the Union, but could be harsh towards troublesome ones! In January 1838 Thomas Lammas escaped from the workhouse, and ended up in Birmingham where he 'enrolled' as a pauper at the Erdington workhouse which served the Aston Union. Erdington was quick to correspond with Bromsgrove stating that Lammas was not their responsibility and that the local workhouse should re-accept him. On the 22nd January 1838 Bromsgrove responded thus "ordered that the overseers of Belbroughton do immediately send for the pauper Thomas Lammas from Erdington workhouse and convey him to the Union workhouse at Bromsgrove." Poor Lammas, however, proved troublesome on his return and a terrible fate awaited him. On the 5th February 1838 the Guardians decreed "ordered that Thomas Lammas, an insane pauper, now in the Union workhouse, be removed and conveyed to the Droitwich Lunatic Asylum."

The Union took a dim view of parental desertions, because, if a father being the only breadwinner in the family, deserted his family then the members would become destitute. Such a family would then have to be relieved either in the workhouse or by outdoor relief, and this would drain the resources of the Union. Cases of desertion were reported quickly, and the Guardians then asked the relieving officer of the district to apprehend the parent and make him pay. There are countless examples in the minute books of such desertions, many of them by fathers who deserted in the winter months when work was scarce. Many hoped that the family would be supported by out relief and not allowed to starve but some of the families were taken to the workhouse instead. The penalty for desertion was severe and included whipping in the early nineteenth century, and later by fines and prison sentences.

Some of the desertions include the following entries -

September 1842 - "Ordered that John Cottrill be empowered to apply to the Justices for a warrant to apprehend George Packwood for deserting his wife and leaving her chargeable to the parish of Bromsgrove."

February 1850 - "Resolved that Richard Burroughs be prosecuted for running away and leaving his wife and child chargeable to the township of Redditch and that D.W. Eaton (clerk) be empowered to take the necessary proceedings in the matter."

July 1850 - "Ordered that Ann May be prosecuted for running away and leaving her child aged 3 years chargeable to the township of Redditch."

September 1852 - "Ordered that Moses Shrimpton of Redditch be prosecuted for running away and leaving Mary Ann his wife and family chargeable to Redditch."

Shrimpton was caught and fined but he deserted his wife and family a second time in May 1864. His story has a tragic ending as he became a well known poacher in the Redditch area and in 1885 he was responsible for the death of a police officer. The attack took place one dark night on P.C. James Davies of Beoley when the officer was ambushed by the poacher who murdered him by slitting his throat! Shrimpton was hunted down, caught and subsequently hanged at Worcester.

In *June 1856* the Board attempted to get the release of a prisoner so that the man could return home to support his family and therefore reduce the costs of the Board - - - "Read a letter from William Wood, a prisoner on board the 'Sterling Castle' hulk (prison ship) whose wife and two children were maintained in the workhouse at the cost of Belbroughton soliciting the Guardians to take certain measures to obtain his release."

In October 1862 Hannah Rutler was prosecuted "for neglecting to support her two illegitimate children now in the workhouse chargeable to Belbroughton."

The year 1862 was a bad one for relief, and the Union became even more tight fisted as shown by this example. The Board received a deputation from the nailers of Bromsgrove complaining of low wages in the district due to the evils of the truck system. The Board was outwardly sympathetic but promised no financial help in the form of outdoor relief, and warned the desperate nailers "to conduct themselves peaceably whilst out of work and that the able bodied, if they became destitute could only be relieved in the workhouse."

The niggardly attitude towards saving money is seen in a large number of miscellaneous examples, e.g. July 19th 1841 - - - "ordered that the master of the workhouse do lay before this Board at the next meeting a statement showing the expense and gain of feeding pigs in the workhouse."

In August 1841 the Board ordered 1 or 2 cwts of old rope from the cheapest source for the employment of the paupers. The Board later sent representatives to the Aston Union to find out how the oakum picking process could be conducted in the workhouse. The scrooge-type attitude for cost cutting is clearly shown in the dietary of the workhouse and by two entries in particular. On November 8th 1841 the quantity of meat to each pauper inmate was reduced from five ounces to four on the special meat days, and the quantity of potatoes was increased instead from half a pound to three quarter pounds on special potato days. Even after this reduction the Board of Guardians still considered itself too generous in its food allocation to paupers and compared itself to other Unions, and as a result produced this astonishing cost cutting exercise sheet. They itemised the price of all food products consumed in one week and divided it by the number of paupers, and they reduced certain items accordingly. The list was as follows:-

October 1842

Provisions	*Cost per head per week*
Flour	8d
Meat	8½d
Cheese	1.2/3d
Potatoes	2d
Oatmeal	½d

Butter	1¼d
Milk	1d
Rice	1/3d
Tea	3/4d
Sugar	1½d
Ale	1.1/3d
Coals	2.3/4d
Candles	¼d
Soap Yellow)	
Soap Mottled)	1.3/4d

In September 1856 the new dietary sheet for pauper children aged 2-9 years was introduced. The reader can draw his own conclusions.

DAY	BREAKFAST			DINNER				SUPPER	
	Bread OZ	Gruel/Milk PT	Pudding Suet or Rice	Soup Pint	Meat Ozs	Bread Ozs	Potatoes Ozs	Bread Ozs	Cheese Ozs
SUNDAY	4 oz	1 pt	8 ozs	–	–	–	–	4 ozs	1 oz
MONDAY	”	”	–	1	–	4	–	”	”
TUESDAY	”	”	–	–	3	–	8	”	”
WEDNESDAY	”	”	–	1	–	4	–	”	”
THURSDAY	”	”	–	–	3	–	8	”	”
FRIDAY	”	”	–	1	–	4	–	”	”
SATURDAY	”	”	–	–	3	–	8	”	”

The Board always adopted a niggardly attitude towards the suppliers to the workhouse - they always wanted the cheapest but the best. In January 1850 they complained against the baker "Mr. Eaton, Relief Officer reported that 11 loaves supplied last week by the contractor were all of them less than 4 lbs and altogether 22 ozs deficient in weight - - - recommended that 9 loaves be sent back." A new contractor was subsequently appointed. In August 1850 they complained against a supplier who refused to accept workhouse products because he considered them inferior "Ordered that if Mr. Perkins, Brush manufacturer of Birmingham persists in his refusal to take the mats which have been made for him by the workhouse inmates the Master of the workhouse do go to Birmingham and endeavour to sell all the mats on hand."

Apparently coal gas arrived in Bromsgrove in the late 1840's and on the 11th September 1850 the Board discussed its merits and costs as a medium of heating and lighting the workhouse. On the 25th of September the Guardians accepted the offer of the Bromsgrove Gas Company to install gas "ordered that gas be introduced into the workhouse - - - the total cost of meter and fittings not to exceed £35.

The fittings were installed; then the Board changed its mind over the cost and continued in a war of attrition with the gas company, haggling over the price of gas. Eventually the gas service was connected but only after the gas company had to lower its price.

In October 1864 the Guardians decided on another way of saving money and agreed to "a box be placed at the Bromsgrove Railway Station for the reception of any used up books and newspapers (discarded by travellers) for the use of the workhouse inmates." The railway company however, turned down such a suggestion.

The working class dreaded the workhouse and did everything possible to stay away from its doors. Final acceptance to the workhouse came as a bitter and heartbreaking experience to a man and his family, and such an experience carried a deep social stigma. The following entry in the minute book for January 1865 makes the point "a letter from Mr. Roger Prosser was read complaining that his name had been mixed up with an application for relief and requesting his name might be erased from the application book and an apology offered him otherwise he should take means to vindicate his character."

The working class regarded the workhouse as a prison, and it was commonly known as a 'bastille', and indeed life within its walls was only marginally better. The tasks for the able bodied paupers; who resented the workhouse most of all, included oakum picking; scrubbing and washing for the women and children and certain old men; and bone breaking and stone breaking for men. Oakum picking involved picking old rope strands and the clean strands were then recycled to make more rope or sacking. Bone breaking was done in order to produce bone dust which was used as a fertilizer by local farmers, and stone breaking was done in order to produce rocks of manageable size and weight which were then used for making roads.

The regimentation and discipline involved sapped patience resulting sometimes in lost tempers and misbehaviour. Such conduct was rarely tolerated and often punished; often in the reduction of the already meagre dietary for a period of two days as illustrated by the following 'General order on Workhouse Rules' (1841) - "It shall be lawful for the master to punish any disorderly pauper by substituting, during a time not greater than 48 hours, for his or her dinner, a meal consisting of 8oz of bread or 1 lb of cooked potatoes and also by withholding from him during the same period all butter, cheese, tea, sugar or broth which such pauper would otherwise receive at any meal during this time."

"It shall be lawful for the Board of Guardians to order

any Refractory pauper to be confined in a separate room, with an alteration of diet as prescribed for Disorderly paupers; but no pauper shall be confined for longer than 24 hours, unless carried before a justice of the peace."

The able bodied poor were those who protested the loudest against the system. Unemployment was the key factor for their demise, but their only relief had to be sought in the workhouse. "First, that except for medical attendance all relief whatever to able bodied persons or to their families, otherwise that in well regulated workhouses shall be declared unlawful, and shall cease; and that all relief afforded in respect of children shall be considered as afforded to their parents - - - -" (Parliamentary Commission 1834). In 1844 the Poor Law Commission ruled that all able bodied including entire families had to go to the workhouse with the following exceptions. Outdoor relief was granted only "on account of sudden and urgent necessity; of any sickness, accident or bodily or mental infirmity; to meet the expenses of the burial of any of their family; to help a widow for the first six months of widowhood; to assist a widow with legitimate children dependent on her; or shall be a wife or child of a soldier or sailor in H.M. Service."

Some workhouses were worse than others, and this was noted by Hippolyte Taine, a French writer in 1874. "I am informed that the able bodied poor prefer their home and freedom at any price. They prefer to be free and to starve. The workhouse is regarded as a prison - - - - the human being becomes a machine treated as if devoid of feeling, insulted quite uncosciously."

The same writer also visited some 'good' workhouses - - - "there is no smell anywhere; the beds are almost white - - - - the most aged and feeble women have white caps and new clothes - - - - we were astounded; this is a palace compared with the kennels in which the poor dwell."

How did life inside the institution affect the paupers? The Chaplain of Holborn workhouse gave this evidence to the Royal Commission in 1905-8. "There is no doubt in my mind that life in the workhouse deteriorates mentally, morally and principally - - - I have seen in countless cases a gradual deterioration of intellect owing to the lack of almost all incentive to use the brain. All necessities of life are provided with no effort on his part - - - -. Often young persons have at first felt their position and surroundings keenly, and yet have shortly found life so congenial that they make no effort to leave; many young people are at first bright and willing to perform the light duties, but under the influence of their associates soon grow lazy and troublesome!

There are many examples of dissent amongst the Bromsgrove workhouse paupers within the period covered by this publication. This dissent often expressed itself in open insubordination. In May 1842 the master complained to the Board about James Lee who on the 17th inst. "endeavoured to excite other paupers to acts of insubordination. The master also reported that he had deprived the pauper of his meat and given him potatoes only for his dinner next day." Another pauper was also punished spending a few days in the isolation room and having his cheese allowance removed for two days.

The year 1842 saw many examples of troublesome behaviour. In October, Thomas Smith flatly refused to work in the workhouse and became verbally abusive and was taken before a magistrate who sent him to jail for 21 days. The Smith episode seems to have been a catalyst, for within the next two months there were several cases of fighting, stealing, indecent behaviour between male and female inmates and abscondences. A number of inmates symbolically tore up their union clothes in a futile gesture against the system. On the 28th November "the master reported having punished Ann Wakeman and Ann Cotton for fighting" (no mention was made of the type of punishment used).

In February 1847 Susan Cashmore was brought before the Board "for maliciously soiling the property of the Guardians by stealing two keys and throwing them into the privy hole." Her punishment was bread and water for one day and solitary confinement for 4 hours.

Emma Portman gained quite a reputation at the workhouse. In July 1847 she was offered work outside the institution but she declined the offer and refused to leave. "Work out of the house having been this day offered to Emma Portman whereby she may maintain herself. Ordered that she be taken before a Justice of the Peace and dealt with according to law if she persists in her refusal to leave the workhouse and neglects to accept the work offered to her before the end of this day week."

Evidently Emma remained in the workhouse and in December she was in trouble yet again. "The master reported that Ann Edwards and Emma Portman had behaved badly in the workhouse." Both were subsequently committed to gaol for 14 days hard labour. In the same month John Taylor, an able bodied inmate misbehaved and he was ordered "to work at breaking stones and on failing to break 3/4 of a yard that he be punished." It was common practice for the house to set this type of work to the indoor paupers, and the Surveyor of Bromsgrove town often supplied large stones to the workhouse and paid 1/- a yard for the inmate to break them into smaller fragments which were then used for road making.

In December 1850 another pauper showed his feelings when he symbolically burned a towel in one of the wards. A few weeks later Joseph Coley was punished for "returning to the workhouse in a drunken and filthy state and that he was placed in the refractory ward during the night. Ordered that he be again placed in the refractory ward for twelve hours with an allowance of bread and water only."

Mary Gibbs seems to have dominated the headlines in the first three months of 1851. She first appeared in the minute book in 1845 when she was listed as a smallpox victim in the workhouse and was nursed back into health. She seems to have been a stable personality and was considered reliable, as she was given a trusted position as an ancilliary nurse at the workhouse. By January 1851, however, a personality change had taken place. She was reprimanded for beating an aged pauper. A few days later she returned to the workhouse in a state of drunkenness after attending a funeral, and when reprimanded she swore and reviled the matron. "The matron also found concealed by Gibbs many articles of food and clothing supposed to belong to the Guardians which, with Gibbs, were brought before the Board." She was found guilty of theft by the magistrate and sentenced to prison for 14 days. Her insolence seems to have signalled a wave of insubordination. Ann Spencer was taken to the refractory ward with an allowance of bread and water in later January 1851 "for maliciously damaging a cushion cover." Several other incidents were reported at the time. On her return to the workhouse from prison Mary Gibbs struck again. "J. Hands complained that Gibbs had threatened to stab his child to the heart - Cashmore and Young (both well known troublemakers) asserted they both heard her say so - - - -. The master of the workhouse reported that Gibbs refused to work ---- admitted she saw the medical officer in the morning and that she did not answer him when he asked her how she was!"

On the 26th March 1851 she was punished for fighting and for refusing to work. She then seems to have settled down until June 30th 1852 when she was reported by the master for destroying an old pair of shoes belonging to the Union.

In May 1851 John Young was in trouble. He had recently left the workhouse because work had been offered him in the town.   However, he returned one night to the workhouse motivated by a mixture of greed and revenge, and was caught stealing lead off the Institution's roof.   He was immediately committed to trial at the next General Quarter Sessions.

The Summer of 1862 saw many desertions of families by fathers, and the Board was under pressure to supply more outdoor relief.   Friction also built up amongst the paupers in the workhouse.   In September three women paupers were taken before the JP for insulting Mrs. Kings the matron and damaging workhouse property.   In late October the trio was in trouble again.   "Eliza Stephenson complained to the Board that she was under fear that Ann Brown and Jane Beresford would do her bodily harm."   Once again they were reported to the JP and reprimanded.   In the same month Hannah Rutter was prosecuted for neglecting to support her two illegitimate children, who were removed into workhouse care.

The period of December 1862 to February 1864 was a particularly bad time for friction and indiscipline in the workhouse, and it revolved around the disastrous appointments of Mr. and Mrs. Pope, master and matron (see chapter on 'Crises').   One of the many incidents involved a Joseph Webb who on the 28th April 1863 went berserk in the workhouse and smashed eight panes of glass.   His punishment confined him to the refractory ward for 24 hours with an allowance of bread and water only.

In the same period the master of the workhouse was threatened by a knife carried by a Richard Gardiner who had a record of mental instability.   He was placed in a separate room with an attendant, and his food was cut up for him and he was only allowed a spoon to eat it with for fear of him doing himself bodily harm.   Dr. Fletcher, the workhouse's medical officer, was also called in to examine the pauper.

There were many who absconded from the workhouse. The Guardians expressed anger at such incidents, but also dismay that paupers had vanished with workhouse property, such as clothing and shoes!   In November 1837 Dianah Wright "absconded from the house with some of the Union clothing, ordered that the master take the necessary steps to have her apprehended."

In March 1842 William Crawford scaled the outer wall and absented himself from the workhouse without leave.   He duly appeared before the Board and the master was instructed to substitute 8ozs of bread instead of his normal dietary for a period of 48 hours.   In May 1847 a John Andrews absconded but was soon sighted and brought back and forfeited his supper and meat for the next day. Often the punishment was a lot harsher than forfeiting one's food. In May 1869 three boys named Reuben Adams, George Taylor and Charles Taylor absconded with workhouse clothing. After their apprehension the master was instructed to flog the three in the presence of the school mistress.

In January 1878 two pauper boys escaped by getting into the garden and climbing over the wall. They subsequently returned and tried to induce other boys to join them, but were caught by the master. The ringleader, Joseph Day, received twelve stripes with the cane as punishment. The Guardians had no pity on those who stole from the workhouse as illustrated by this entry of the 30th January 1850. "The master of the workhouse reported that John Young had carried away from the workhouse a pair of shoes, the property of the Union, and that he and Richard Band had sold them; that Band was in custody and that Young had absconded from the workhouse together with William Lashford taking with them the clothes of the Union. Ordered that the law takes its course as regards Young and Band for stealing the shoes and that Young and Lashford be prosecuted for absconding from the workhouse and carrying away the Union clothes."

A number of paupers were reprimanded for taking food from the workhouse kitchen without consent, and in February 1838 Anne Price complained to a visiting committee that she did not receive enough bread to eat. Apparently the master and matron took exception to this and Anne was punished without Guardian consent. Later Anne Price confessed to the Board that other paupers had put her up to the complaint. The Board pardoned the master for his treatment of the pauper.

Sometimes life in the workhouse became too much to bear hence the outbursts of violence, and sadly some paupers even contemplated suicide. In June 1843 an inmate by the name of Thomas Jones made an unsuccessful attempt on his own life, claiming "that he was tired of life and no longer wished to live." The Guardians immediately called the workhouse chaplain to see to the poor man's emotional and spiritual needs. In April 1870 a Joseph Harris, also an inmate, hanged himself in the workhouse. The medical officer of health was blamed for not removing the man at an earlier date to the Powick asylum.

In the early years the visiting committee comprised of local middle class people who regarded themselves as kind, considerate and God-fearing. Later in the century members of the Guardian group also served on the committee.

The Visiting Committee took upon themselves to visit the workhouse on a regular basis and to act independently and objectively. They would talk to the pauper inmates and often listen to their complaints, and they then reported some of these to the Board. They would also suggest remedies and actions for the Board to take. The Visiting Committee had no real power and could not compel the Guardians to act, but their recommendations, nevertheless, were nearly always followed.

One of the first visits took place in February 1838. The Committee listened to the complaint of Anne Price, pauper, who claimed that she didn't have enough to eat. She later confessed to the Guardians that others had put her up to it. The Committee also recommended that the workhouse "should buy spinning wheels and that paupers should be employed in spinning mops." Nothing came of this suggestions and the Board soon turned to the soul destroying occupation for the pauper inmates of oakum picking, the task stipulated by the Poor Law Commissioners in London.

In July 1838 the Visiting Committee's suggestion that the union should supply inmates with prayer books and testaments was followed. By the 1840's the Committee's duties seemed to have been mainly diverted to that of checking the state of the workhouse building. In April 1847 the Committee recommended that the yards be levelled and in part re-gravelled, and also asked that the baths be repaired and also one of the drains. In July 1847 they requested whitewashing of the water closets and the laying of a new bathroom floor. In August 1847 they recommended that part of the building be whitewashed with Bristol lime including the sleeping wards, the rooms within the hospital block, mens' day room, school room, kitchen, dining room, larder and passages. In May 1857 they requested that doors, windows and frames be well cleaned, and that the master should also make out a list of the painting and repairs that were necessary - also that the chimney piece in the master's room be repaired and that the pumps be examined. In August 1857 the Visiting Committee, after viewing the hospital were all agreed that an additional window should be placed in each of the two middle rooms on the ground floor.

Occasionally, however, the Visiting Committee did press forthright opinions on sensitive and important issues as was the case in June 1858. Mr. Fletcher, the Medical Officer of the workhouse, who was a very capable practitioner had his professional judgement questioned. "Mr. Fletcher reported in writing that Ann Harris an inmate of the workhouse is very insane and threatens to murder other inmates if they keep her in bed at nights." Ann Harris was questioned by the Committee and they found the woman completely sane, and informed the Guardians so. In October 1859 the Committee looked at the provision for schooling in the workhouse - - - "recommended that an easel be put up in the school and a series of broad sheets for the younger children be made." The new chaplain, the Rev. Kingdom amplified the request and asked for a few books on the Catechism be provided also. In the same month the Committee suggested that one of the workhouse yards be rolled and asked for the salting tub be given a new bottom of lead. In June 1862 the Committee made a strange request to the Board, that two breeding pigs be bought. The aim was to improve the self-sufficiency of the workhouse by providing it with a supply of ready meat. In April 1862 workhouse grown produce such as pig meat, vegetables and potatoes raised £11-17s-6d.

From the late 1860's the Visiting Committee seems to have been redirected to the more mundane matters of workhouse life. In July 1864 they requested that the boys playroom floor be repaired and the ceiling to the staircase in the hospital be altered. In the same month they asked for three tin dishes to be provided and a sample of hats for pauper men to be produced. In July 1865 the Committee "ordered that the cooking range, the boilers and laundry stove and water cocks be repaired and that tenders be sent in the next Board Day for painting the kitchen and that Mr. Brewster be requested to purchase a mangle for the workhouse." The tender for £4, the lowest one, was subsequently accepted by the thrifty Board.

Other Committees were also formed by the Guardians, and one of these was briefed to examine the care of Bromsgrove Union mentally ill paupers who were moved to local asylums.

The attitude of the Board towards the asylum was a strange one at first. There is evidence to suggest that the Guardians sometimes offloaded troublesome inmates on to the local asylums as punishment and at other times displayed a more caring and sympathetic view towards this unfortunate group of paupers. However, the detached and thrify attitude is clearly seen in the early years as the Guardians decided regularly to send the mentally ill to the cheapest asylum in the area. On the 9th July 1838 the Guardians moved Rebecca Mason and John Frier from the local asylum at Droitwich to Stafford asylum because the charges there were lower. Their dissatisfaction was aroused by the receipt of a bill for the maintenance of the insane at Droitwich in December 1837 which came to a quarterly sum of £35-3s-2d. The vindictive attitude of the Board in moving unwanted and troublesome paupers from the workhouse to the asylum is illustrated by the case of John Morrison, an able-bodied pauper in September 1838, who maybe feigned madness in order to thwart the Board's plan to deport him to Ireland. Instead the poor man was declared a lunatic and moved to the Droitwich asylum where his upkeep was paid for out of County rates, and not from the parish relief fund. The second such case is provided by Thomas Lammas who absconded from the Bromsgrove institution in January 1838 and enrolled as an inmate of Erdington Workhouse, before the Birmingham Union forcibly sent him back to Belbroughton, the parish of his birth and thus back to the Union workhouse at Bromsgrove. On his return he again proved troublesome and was unceremoniously moved on the order of the Guardians to the Droitwich lunatic asylum. During a bad period of insubordination in the workhouse in the months of September to November 1842 a number of paupers were transferred to asylums. Sometimes the transfer was blocked as was the case of Charles Woodhouse who was sent on trial at the Petty Sessions in Wolverhampton by the Board. The court considered the man sane and refused to sign an order for his admission to the Staffordshire Lunatic Asylum.

There were incidents of return transfers from the asylum to the Bromsgrove workhouse. In November 1840 William Parkes of Belbroughton recovered after treatment and was re-admitted into the workhouse. In August 1848 Ann Smallwood, a lunatic at Bethnall Green Lunatic Asylum, London was released and returned to Bromsgrove. On the 27th May 1890 a William Gardner was discharged from Powick Asylum and re-admitted to the workhouse.

There were, however, many examples of the Board's dissatisfaction with the asylums, claiming that the patients should not have been released back to their care at Bromsgrove. Indeed the asylums did have many failures as witnessed by this entry of the 9th August 1866 - - - "reported the removal of William Jones, a criminal lunatic from the asylum to the county gaol at Worcester." Sometimes the Board itself failed to diagnose a mentally ill pauper until it was late as was the case of Joseph Harris who hanged himself at the workhouse on the 22nd April 1870, or was the poor man suffering from acute depression brought on suddenly by his recent admission? A similar incident occurred on the 24th June 1873 when a pauper from the union hanged himself at the Powick Lunatic Asylum shortly after his admission there. A more humane spirit was exercised by the Board in June 1865 when a committee was appointed to visit the County Lunatic Asylum at Powick and to enquire into the general health and progress of its inmates. There were 29 lunatics chargeable to the union at the time of the visit, and the Committee's subsequent report included the following observation - - - "they all appear to be exceedingly well cared for, a large majority of them are old and confirmed cases - - - - and that five of them were sufficiently recovered to return to the workhouse." In July 1866 another Visiting Committee was conducted when there were 42 lunatics registered to the Bromsgrove Union. In August 1873 another group of Guardians visited Powick where there were 45 mentally ill registered to the Union, and only six of these, it was claimed had any real hope of recovery.

The Guardians were impressed with the way the paupers were looked after - - - "the establishment which appears to be exceedingly well managed - - - the inmates clean and well cared for - - - and everything provided which may conduce to their comfort and happiness."

Another visit by the Committee took place in July 1890 - - - "we saw and examined all the patients chargeable to this union viz. 33 males and 44 females a total of 77 patients who in every case were clean and appeared well cared."

By 1890 the Powick Asylum was suffering from overcrowding. In June 1891 the male lunatic ward was full and a local patient from Bromsgrove had to be transferred to the Joint Counties Lunatic Asylum at Abergavenny, Wales. In November 1891 owing to the crowded state of the male division another Union patient had to be removed to Derby Borough Asylum.

The lack of asylum space worsened and in March 1899 the County Council declared its intention of building an additional County Council Lunatic Asylum on the north-western boundary of the county. The Guardians at Bromsgrove opposed the idea - - - "that such a site is unfavourably situated from access from a large part of this Union and that it is advisable that a site more accessible from the north-eastern part of the county be procured." The eventual site was to be in Bromsgrove itself. The council bought up the Barnsley Hall Estate for £17,000; once the property of the well known Barnsley family. The new Worcestershire Mental Hospital was opened on the site in 1903 to hold 570 patients, and was named Barnsley Hall Hospital.

The following extract was enshrined in the legislation that set up the 1834 workhouse system. "The paupers situation shall not be made as eligible as that of the independent labourer of the lowest class.   The evidence shows that as the condition of any pauper class is raised above that of independent labourers, the condition of the independent class is depressed, their industry impaired, their employment becomes unsteady and their wages diminished.   Such persons are therefore under the strongest inducements to quit the less eligible class of labourer and enter the more eligible class of paupers.   Every penny bestowed that renders the position of the pauper more eligible than that of the independent labourer is a bounty on indolence and vice."

Barnsley Hall, Bromsgrove.   The new Worcestershire Mental Hospital was opened in 1903 to hold 570 patients.

Many examples of the above attitude have already been included in the book.   However, there are a few examples of the Board's humanity in the period covered by this publication, and most of these tend to appear in the later years especially after 1860.

Generally the Guardians were niggardly when it came to the question of outdoor relief, and preferred to threaten the unemployed with the workhouse unless they made determined attempts to find work.   However, some compassion was shown at times as shown by the following entries in the minute books:-

November 9th 1840 - - - "that William Wakeman is suffering from a bad leg, that the wives of John Wheeler, Joseph Amos and Robert Byng are confined and that Thomas Lloyd's wife has rheumatism, and in consequence wholly unable to follow their usual employment. Ordered that such relief be given to them."

December 28th 1840 - - - "that Mary Oldfield has consumption (T.B.), Elizabeth Harris, burns, Sarah Oakes, fever, Sarah wife of Thomas Bridgewater, confinement, Ann Bruce a bad hand and William Guise, accident, and Thomas Heely, fever. Ordered that such relief be given to them."

January 25th 1841 "Thomas Hawkins aged 50, an able bodied man residing in and belonging to Tardebigge, a widower having applied to this Board for outdoor relief until the weather breaks; he being unable to follow his usual employment of brickmaking in consequence of the frost and to procure other work, and he having 11 children at home only one of whom is able to maintain himself at the present time, four partially and six being wholly dependent on their father for support. The Board considering this a case of emergency and one sufficiently urgent to justify them in departing from the Rule of the Poor Commission prohibiting outdoor relief from being given to any able bodied person. Order that relief be given to Thomas Hawkins to the amount of twenty shillings by 8 weekly instalments by way of a loan."

The Guardians had to seek the permission from the Poor Law Commissioners in London whom they held in great awe and esteem. The latter reluctantly agreed to the giving of outrelief, no doubt realising that it was cheaper in the long term to grant a loan than force the entire family of twelve into the workhouse. In November 1841 the Guardians once again sanctioned outrelief - - - "The wife of Mr. T. Gibbs an able bodied agricultural labourer, having applied to this Board for relief on account of the insufficiency of his earnings for the maintenance of himself and wife and five children aged respectively 8, 7, 5, 3 and 2. Ordered that 5 loaves of bread be given to them weekly for 2 weeks the case being considered one of emergency and that our clerk report the same to the Poor Law Commissioners for their approval."

In April 1842 the Board was prepared to employ some of the nailers to produce nails and pay them out of rates until better times. However, the Guardians were overruled by the Commissioners who ordered the poor nailers to break stones instead. Later, and more by coincidence than design the broken stones were put into good use in surfacing a local turnpike road.

In July 1852 the Guardians financed emigration at a time when a large number of local paupers expressed their desire to leave Britain. Five families were eventually selected by the Board for special financial help in paying towards their passage costs. The Poor Law Commission sanctioned this.

In September 1857 Benjamin Duffins, an able bodied pauper, was allowed to leave the workhouse with his two eldest children and was given 2s/6d and permission to leave the youngest child in the workhouse until his situation had improved at work.

In August 1862 a woman inmate went berserk in the workhouse and normally such behaviour would have been punished most severely but the Guardians exercised leniency and compassion - - - "The master reported that Ann Brown had wilfully broken several panes of glass in the womens ward - no punishment to be inflicted because the master refused to allow her to see her child." The master was reprimanded and his attention was drawn to his contract and to observe the eighth regulation of Article 99 of the General Consolidated Order. The same compassion is again seen in August 1863 when Richard Gardiner a pauper inmate who was suffering from a very bad skin complaint was taken repeatedly over a period of two weeks to Droitwich brine baths. In November 1864 the Board again showed some compassion when they made this ruling "ordered that a cheap bath chair be got and in proper weather any of the disabled but well behaved paupers of the workhouse be occasionally taken out into the garden in it."

In July 1887 the Board leased a piece of land as a playground for the pauper children, and cricket materials were bought for the children to play with. Such a decision as this would have been unheard of fifty years earlier. In March 1889 thirty-seven able bodied male persons were in receipt of outrelief, and reasons included coffin and fees for dead wife, sickness of self, accident injury to foot, sickness of wife and sickness of children. In the 1890's the Board's attitude had mellowed yet again as shown by these three extracts.

August 1892 "On the suggestion of the Chairman it was ordered that the master do procure a supply of eye guards for the vagrants breaking stones - also suggested that wood chopping should be substituted instead of stone breaking."

November 1892 "Ordered to allow 1oz of tobacco and ½oz of snuff to be given to such of the workhouse inmates who are able bodied who are employed upon the work of a specially disagreeable character."

August 1895 "Decided that the Board challenge the members of the Bromsgrove Urban District Council to play a cricket match - the gate money to be handed over to the poor relief fund."

Such extracts as these were surely a sign of enlightened times. Incidentally, the Council accepted the cricket challenge and a total of £4-16s-0d was raised from the public gate, but no mention of the result of the match appears in the minute books!

The Board relaxed certain rules on special national occasions. In February 1863 the workhouse paupers were allowed the same extra rations as those granted on Xmas days; the reason being the celebrations associated with the marriage of the Prince of Wales, the future Edward VII. Most Christmases in the later years of the nineteenth century were regarded as special occasions for the paupers, unlike the early years when a scrooge attitude was very prevalent. In December 1872 the Board announced "ordered that the usual Christmas fare be allowed to the inmates of the workhouse; also that an offer made by the Bromsgrove Amateur Dramatic Society to give an entertainment for the inmates and ratepayers in the Dining Hall of the workhouse be accepted." In December 1894 "it was resolved that the inmates of the workhouse be given roast beef and plum pudding on Xmas day with the usual supply of ale, tobacco and snuff and fruit etc." In the same festive week an invitation was read for the inmates of the workhouse to attend a play at the Drill Hall on the 27th inst. by the Amateur Dramatic Society.

The Board of Guardians were very loyal to parliament and especially so to the crown. In March 1882 an attempt was made on the life of Queen Victoria and the Guardians sent her the following message - - - "it was unanimously resolved that a message of congratulations be forwarded to the Queen expressing our thankfulness at Her Majesty's escape from the recent dastardly attempt against her life." The Board was deeply touched by her response which came from Whitehall on the 5th April 1882 sent by her private secretary - - - "that Her Majesty is deeply sensible of the loyalty and affection of her faithful subjects." Further opportunity for celebration came in June 1887 with the fiftieth anniversary of the accession of the Queen. This time the inmates once again were to benefit - - - "the paupers to have roast beef and plum pudding for dinner, tea, coffee, bread and butter and cake for tea and for supper coffee and cake with bread and butter or bread and cheese - - - also that a similar quantity of beer and tobacco and snuff to that supplied at Christmas be given." The inmates were also allowed to attend a dramatic entertainment at the Bromsgrove recreation ground on the 22nd June 1887.

The Board was always anxious to instill Christian virtues into the pauper inmates and every effort was made by the Guardians to integrate paupers into the local religious community. In July 1892 Mr. Lewis, a Guardian, proposed "that the chaplain be asked to give the invitation to the tramps to attend Divine Service on Sundays. Mr. Allcock seconded." Permission was also given at this time to the workhouse children to attend Sunday Schools in the town of Bromsgrove and "it was resolved that the children be allowed to attend the annual treat of the All Saints Sunday School on the 18th July 1892 and also to attend the annual treat of the Bromsgrove Sunday School Union on the 28th July 1892." In November 1894 the master submitted a letter to the Board he had received from the Rev. F.L. Milward asking that the workhouse children over 9 years of age be allowed to attend the Band of Hope recently started at All Saints School room. The Guardians agreed immediately to the request.

By the 1890's the Board's change of heart towards the paupers in its care can be clearly seen also in the way the Guardians improved the social and cultural life within the workhouse. In the early years the workhouse was often regarded a bleak, inhospitable and harsh institution, but by the last decade of the century the workhouse was becoming more bearable for some of its inmates. The Guardians welcomed approaches from members of the local community who were offering their services. One of these caring persons was the Reverend J.W. Comfort who wrote the following letter to the Chairman of the Guardians in November 1891.

"Dear Sir,

I find upon enquiring that there is an almost entire absence of newspapers and magazines and literature for the inmates of the workhouse.

With a view of supplying the inmates with newspaper reading I have obtained a box which will be placed in a conspicuous part of the town and in which many of our townspeople will, I believe, gladly deposit current copies of daily papers, magazines etc. May I ask the Guardians to give directions to one of the inmates to clear the box say every other day. I am prepared also to make arrangements to give the inmates of the workhouse an entertainment of vocal and instrumental music and occasionally a series of magic lantern views on one evening each week during the winter and I beg through you to ask the Guardians' permission to do so. I trust indeed that it will be granted, for one musical evening per week cannot fail to bring much pleasure into the lives of many of the poor under your care and it will awaken in those who take part a healthy interest in their welfare."

The Board agreed to this request and even appointed a small committee to look into the organization.

In July 1892 the Board's generosity was in evidence again when they agreed to allow old people and children to attend Gunnett's Circus in the town, after receiving an invitation from a local townslady. In January 1895 the Board once again accepted help from the community when "the master also reported that Miss Gay had presented 24 books from the Religious Tract Society towards the formation of a library at the workhouse."

CHAPTER FIVE

CRISES

1. The Reverend Gray incident of 1838.
2. The death of Henry Cartwright 1842.
3. Instability at the helm 1848.
4. The cholera epidemic 1849.
5. The Mr. and Mrs. Pope chapter 1863.
6. The dietary scandals of 1859 and 1868.
7. The death of Sarah Jane Ward 1899.

The first crisis came early in the history of the Bromsgrove Workhouse, and came as a result of the early opposition to the 1834 Act and its unsympathetic view towards the able bodied poor. There was a deep seated feeling throughout the country and it manifested itself in the form of riots in the industrial counties of the north of England. The main issue was the balance between outdoor relief and indoor relief, and the new workhouses were the institutions of indoor relief. Poor people expected out relief in the form of food or money at home not the workhouse, and to be refused outrelief and directed to the dreaded institution was, for many, the end of all hope.

The local scandal took place in early November 1838 and hit the Guardians very hard. The incident concerned the removal to the workhouse of two elderly women; Susan Morris and Ann Bunce. The Rev. G.R. Gray condemned the Board for forcing the two women against their will to leave their homes and enter the institution. His attack was conducted in letters to the Board and to the local and national newspapers; and virtually accused the Guardians of kidnapping the two unfortunate women. The Guardians were incensed by the charge and declared "that the two women were infirm, destitute and in a filthy condition, deserted by their own families and unable to provide the necessary comforts. Ann Bunce being also in a state of total blindness!" The Rev. Gray persisted in his attack, especially against the Chairman of the Board of Guardians, George

Francis Iddins, and maybe it was this personal dislike that fired Gray's condemnations.   Gray intensified his crusade when his hostile letter was published in the 'Guardian' newspaper in late November, as a result of which the Guardians immediately called a special meeting on the 25th November and accused Gray "of a very gross perversion of the facts", and went into the counter-attack by sending a defending letter containing all the facts of the case to all the Worcester newspapers.   Undaunted the Rev. Gray refused to be silenced, and the deeply embarrassed Guardians sought advice from the London based Commissioners of the New Poor Law Amendment Act.   The episode even reached the Attorney General before the dust finally settled on the matter.   The whole incident gave the workhouse a very bad image at a very sensitive time in its development.   The Union was also hurt, where it hurst most; in its pocket for the whole case had cost them £27.-7s-3d. to defend their 'honour'.

The second scandal to hit the Guardians came four years later in January 1842, when Henry Cartwright aged five and an inmate of the workhouse died as a result of the negligence of Dr. Fletcher the Medical Officer of Health.   Fletcher is portrayed in the many minute books as a caring and hard working individual who was always keen to promote the interests and welfare of the paupers, and the incident came as a tragic shock to him.   The workhouse inmates were all suffering from the highly contagious skin complaint, known then as the 'itch'.   The well tried cure for this rash was to give the body a liberal treatment of sulphur of potassium, but it appears that young Cartwright received too much of a dosage as the official entry in the minute book records "We find that the deceased Henry Cartwright came to his death in consequence of his being immersed in a solution of sulphur of potassium as a cure for the itch and we consider the conduct of Mr. Fletcher, the surgeon under whose direction it was applied as injudicious and negligent." The doctor was duly admonished by the Board, but in view of his good and loyal service in the area he was allowed to retain his post.

In May 1847 another death provoked a crisis in the ranks of the Guardians.   A pauper by the name of William Bartlam was removed from Alvechurch to the workhouse and died within a day of acute inflammation of the lungs.   It was the opinion of the Board that the man should not have been brought in whilst in that state and the respective relieving officer and churchwarden were severely reprimanded for the whole incident once again brought discredit upon the Bromsgrove 'house', and served as a reminder of the 'Gray' incident of 1838.

An internal dispute amongst the Guardians revealed a division in their ranks, and caused some instability in the Summer of 1848. It was as a result of the death of their Chairman, George Francis Iddins Esq., and the subsequent elections for a replacement. It was contested between Mr. Wylde, the vice chairman and Lord Lyttleton, Lord Lieutenant of the County and serving Guardian. Mr. Wylde emerged the victor but within two weeks he had resigned, apparently on the grounds of ill health. This prompted a second election which was won by Lord Lyttleton, and Mr. Greening the loser was duly elected the new vice chairman. The Guardians rarely agreed unanimously on most issues, and these differences nearly always manifested themselves in the appointment of workhouse staff over the years.

One of the greatest crises to face the Board came in August to October 1849 when cholera broke out in the area. The 'Nuisances removal and diseases Preventation Act' of the previous year had considerably widened and increased the powers of the Board, and also added to its workload. Quite a few people were prosecuted in the area as a result, one of the first being Samuel Bray of Stoke Prior on the account of his cesspools which posed a danger to public health. Even the prominent Clive family, lord of the manor of Redditch, was warned over a particular nuisance. The cholera, however, despite fines and warnings, came in mid August 1849 and the first outbreak was recorded in Stoke Heath in the home of the Knight family. Here Dr. Fletcher, the M.O.H. "found five holes full of putrid stinking water, one privy for five families and one pump, the water of which was affected by a large cesspool near to the well". On the 29th August the M.O.H. reported "the death of Charlotte Willis, her daughter and Paul Bartleet at Stoke Prior of Asiatic cholera." The entry continued "George Willis having cholera symptoms to be moved to the place of Refuge, Bromsgrove - that several other persons were suffering from diarrhoea - that he (Fletcher) had removed the families of such persons and ordered the soiled linen to be destroyed". Cholera spread quickly in the neighbourhood, and panic ensued during September and October. An entry of October 3rd reads "Mr. Fletcher reported to the Board that cholera had again appeared at the Imperial Works, Stoke Prior with extreme virulence, and that several deaths had taken place". Seven days later another entry "Mr. Fletcher reported that two cholera cases have occurred this week in Holy Lane in the centre of the town of Bromsgrove and that they evidently arose from a privy situated at the back of the houses". Between August 1st and the 24th October 1849, Mr. Fletcher attended twenty-two cases of cholera and four hundred and twenty five severe cases of diarrhoea. The other four medical officers working the Board's area were also fully stretched. At the end of the crisis in late October the Board of Guardians gave its official thanks to Dr. Fletcher and the other officials for their hard work, but the thanks were not matched by financial reward and even the loyal and hard working Fletcher's claims for expenses were not met in full by the thrifty Board.

BLUE STAGE OF THE SPASMODIC CHOLERA.
Sketch of a Girl who died of Cholera, in Sunderland, November, 1831.
Published at the Lancet Office, 29 Strand.

A Cholera victim

The worst crisis experienced by the Guardians came in 1862 and involved their unwise choice of staff. Their decision brought the workhouse to its knees. In December 1862 Mr. Rose, the workhouse Master and Mrs. Kings, the matron resigned their posts, the latter had served the Union well for eighteen years. The Board placed advertisements in the local press "That the advertisement giving notice of such appointments be inserted once in the 'Midland Counties Herald', 'Worcester Herald', 'Bromsgrove Messenger' and 'Redditch Indicator', the joint salary to be £80 a year with furnished apartments and such provisions as the house affords - preference to be given to a married couple without incumbrance." The well advertised posts attracted eight sets of applications, including that of Mr. and Mrs. Hill, master and matron of the Stourbridge Union Workhouse. After some disagreement, the Board appointed Mr. and Mrs. Pope, the master and schoolmistress of the Penkridge Union Workhouse. Mr. Pope was to receive a salary of £50 p.a. and his wife as the new matron was to receive £30 p.a. Within a short period of time the Guardians were ruefully regretting their choice, as the new couple soon became unpopular amongst inmates and fellow staff. Both were abrasive in their manner especially Mrs. Pope who had a reputation for a hurtful tongue and domineering attitude. During the next fifteen months the workhouse was to experience a major breakdown in control, and increasing friction and indiscipline amongst the inmates and declining morale amongst the staff. There are many examples of indiscipline, the first reported proved to be the catalyst for the others. Martin McMain, an able bodied pauper, in March 1863 refused to leave the workhouse on work being offered to him - - - "ordered that he be required to break a yard and a half of pebbles a day and if he fails to perform this task of work, that the Master be empowered to take him before the J.P. with a view to his being punished".

In April 1863 Joseph Webb went berserk in the Workhouse and smashed up eighteen panes of glass. Furthermore, McMain's conduct deteriorated and in June 1863 he was committed to Worcester prison for twenty-one days. The uneasy atmosphere was compounded by the arrival of smallpox in Bromsgrove in June 1863. It was the formidable Mrs. Pope who created the greatest unrest. Friction built up between her and Miss Dance the schoolmistress almost from the day of arrival of the new matron. Mrs. Pope was the schoolmistress at Penkridge and greatly interfered in Miss Dance's role, even criticising her in the presence of the inmates. In October 1863 the Board, by then increasingly concerned, issued a veiled threat to both ladies and called in an inspector to look into the cause of the friction. The inspector urged the two to adhere to their own duties, a clear hint to Mrs. Pope to mind her own business. This reprimand did nothing to defuse the situation, and Mrs. Pope seems to have declared unofficial war on the poor school teacher by the end of the month. The result was that Miss Dance's confidence was soon shattered, and she lost control of her class and her low morale quickly led to a nervous breakdown. Eleven children were reported to the Board by Mr. Pope for bad behaviour in the classroom, and the Guardians had to take harsh action to stamp out the unrest amongst the pauper boys and ordered the Master to threaten the boys with the birch if their behaviour did not improve. Subsequently one boy was indeed thrashed with the birch, and this measure seems to have broken the rebellion. The

Guardians were in despair at the situation and on the tenth of November 1863 a motion was hurriedly passed. "Resolved that the Poor Law Board be informed that the workhouse continues in a very disturbed and unsatisfactory state - that there is an increased amount of insubordination growing up amongst the inmates, occasioned as the Guardians believe from the hatred and ill-feeling existing between the Matron and the schoolmistress, and the Guardians are of the opinion that good order and regularity will not be brought about until one or both of these officers are removed by resignation or by dismissal. The Matron, and observations recently made by her with reference to the schoolmistress, the Board consider improper and injudicious - namely to one of the inmates "Did you see old Dame Dance come in this morning; she has been out all night . . . ."

On the same day as the motion the Master reported that the porter had grossly insulted him. The porter was immediately forced to resign and a Mr. Gould was appointed as a replacement at £15 p.a. The crisis was provoked further in November by an outbreak of diarrhoea amongst the pauper inmates.

In January 1864 the Board's purge was put into action and they demanded Mrs. Pope's resignation as Matron . . . . . "that experience has shown that Mrs. Pope owing to her temper and misdemeanour is unable to enforce and preserve due subordination and discipline amongst the officers and inmates of the workhouse and that she has in consequence forfeited the confidence of the Guardians. Under these circumstances the Board cannot consent to Mrs. Pope's continuance in office and they accordingly request that the Guardians will call upon her to place her resignation in their hands". Miss Dance was also asked to hand in her resignation. In fact all three officers tended their resignations including the master. The purge was a success and the workhouse soon settled down to normality. The three posts were advertised and seven sets applied for the master-matron vacancy, and three applications were received for the schoolmistress post. The Guardians failed once again to make a unanimous choice for the key posts and eventually a compromise appointment was made. Mr. & Mrs. Danks were appointed and a Miss Elizabeth Sheppard was appointed as the new schoolmistress. The latter did not stay long and had to resign on the grounds of ill health in May 1865, and was replaced by Miss Mary Porter from the Cheadle Union.

The quality and quantity of food in the Bromsgrove Workhouse dietary provoked crisis in 1859 and 1868. The inmates received the minimum of food because the aim of all these Victorian workhouses was to save money and deter paupers from applying for indoor relief (the workhouse test). The dietary at Bromsgrove remained unchanged from 1838 to 1859 and was similar to the following:-

Breakfast			Dinner		
Men	-	5 ozs bread	Men	-	6 ozs bread
		1½ pints gruel			1 oz cheese
Women	-	4 ozs bread	Women	-	5 ozs bread
		1½ pints gruel			1 oz cheese

Supper

Men	-	5 ozs bread
		1 oz cheese
Women	-	4 ozs bread
		1 oz cheese

Meagre amounts of meat were sometimes given, and some small portions of potatoe pie, peas and vegetables.

Dr. Fletcher the Medical Officer for the workhouse and M.O.H. for Bromsgrove had frequently disagreed with the meagre rations, and on the 25th January 1859 the first scandal happened and was duly chronicled in the minute book "Read a letter from Mr. Fletcher M.O.H. stating that he had been informed that James Clarke an inmate had eaten some of the flesh and marrow of the leg of a horse (bone breaking was a regular occupation of the inmates) and that in Mr. Fletcher's opinion he did it for hunger. James Clarke appeared before the Board and stated that he broke a bone and ate some of the marrow believing it to be a cow-bone but he did not do it from hunger". This is the only reference to this dramatic incident, one so similar to scandalous Andover incident of 1845 which drew such widespread national criticism from a hostile press. The Board of Guardians at Bromsgrove Workhouse must have worked feverishly and successfully to hide the whole incident from the local press.

Nine years were to elapse before Dr. Fletcher raised the issue of the dietary once again when he submitted an improved dietary to the Poor Law Board in London which he reinforced with this letter to the Bromsgrove Guardians.

Bromsgrove,
22nd September 1868

My Lord and Gentlemen,

Mr. Humphries (Clerk of the Union) has given me the letter from the Poor Law Commissioners respecting the proposed dietary -

My attention was first called to the insufficiency of the

present dietary by an idiot eating gravel because he was hungry. -

Before recommending any improvement in it I lived a week (in the year 1837) on the Workhouse diet for the able bodied inmates -

My cravings of hunger were more than I could possibly have imagined or can describe - I have since known the inmates as well as the idiots eat putrid horseflesh and oil cake intended for the dogs and others have devoured their poulticies -

The quantity of meat per week (¾lb a pound) the able-bodied now have and I recommend is only a fraction more than *a tenth part* of what the convict or soldier has -

To reduce the quantity of meat to ½ a pound per week, or 1/14th of that given to our Convicts and Soldiers must indeed be reducing the dietary to a painful and dangerous standard.

I see no objections to the other suggestions of the Poor Law Commissioners.

Signed Dr. Fletcher.

The Poor Law Board was taken aback by Fletcher's letters especially by his correspondence dated November 2nd 1868 which included a pointed attack on the workhouse dietary . . . . . .
"it is certainly below the dietary given to criminals in our county jail". The Poor Law Board asked Dr. Fletcher to be specific and to actually list food that was most deficient in the dietary. On the 1st December 1868 Dr. Fletcher, who was by that time clearly running out of patience with the stalling tactics of officialdom replied curtly "If the commissioners wish me to state what article I consider the present dietary is most deficient of, I should say Bread!" An outbreak of diarrhoea took place within a few days of this letter, and Dr. Fletcher took the initiative and requested that the Bromsgrove Guardians include more bread immediately in the dietary "and not have it substituted by either vegetables or peas". As a result of Fletcher's dialogue with London, the Poor Law Board suggested new guidelines for workhouse dietaries which were a compromise with Fletcher's suggested dietary . . . "that two dinners of soup to be given, not three, in a week to the aged and infirm and children in the workhouse . . . . they (Poor Law Board) also doubt the expediency of giving meat so frequently to the able bodied - perhaps for one of the meat dinners, a dinner of suet pudding might be substituted - That it appeared that one pint of rice milk was to be allowed to the aged and

infirm at breakfast, and ¾ pint of cocoa at supper - the Board suggested that tea should be given to the aged and infirm at those meals except to those who may prefer rice milk at one of them - That as regards the allowance of butter at supper, the Board considered ½ oz sufficient and suggested that it might be substituted for the quantity named in the table".

The outcome therefore was a small success for Dr. Fletcher's initiative and determination. Fletcher was a well respected officer of the Bromsgrove Union having displayed a humane touch when others in authority had remained aloof and unsympathetic to the problems of the poor. He was to end his career of thirty years in October 1872.

In August 1885 the workhouse dietary was amended yet again. The reader can judge for oneself the quality and variety on offer.

DIETARY FOR THE ABLE BODIED   AUGUST 1885.

	BREAKFAST		DINNER					SUPPER		
	Bread	Gruel	Cooked Meat	Potatoes	Bread	Soup	Rice or Suet Pudding	Bread	Cheese	Broth
	ozs.	pts.	ozs.	ozs.	ozs.	pts.	ozs.	ozs.	ozs.	pts.
Sun. Men	6	1½	—	—	—	—	14	6	2	—
Women	5	1½	—	—	—	—	12	5	2	—
Mon. Men	6	1½	—	—	4	1½	—	6	2	—
Women	5	1½	—	—	4	1½	—	5	2	—
Tues. Men	6	1½	4	12	—	—	—	6	—	1½
Women	5	1½	4	12	—	—	—	5	—	1½
Wed. Men	6	1½	—	—	4	1½	—	6	2	—
Women	5	1½	—	—	4	1½	—	5	2	—
Thur. Men	6	1½	4	12	—	—	—	6	—	1½
Women	5	1½	4	12	—	—	—	5	—	1½
Fri. Men	6	1½	—	—	4	1½	—	6	2	—
Women	5	1½	—	—	4	1½	—	5	2	—
Sat. Men	6	1½	4	12	—	—	—	6	—	1½
Women	5	1½	4	12	—	—	—	5	—	1½

The dietary for the aged, infirm and imbeciles was similar with marginally smaller portions of potatoes. They did not receive gruel and broth and cheese, but did receive rations of tea and butter.

A tragic death in the Workhouse in January 1899 provoked a crisis for the Guardians. Sarah Jane Ward, aged six and a half years, and an inmate of the house died of horrific burns on the 28th January. The Guardians were sent a report from the deputy coroner on the 31st inst., based on his study of the body of the poor child. The letter also contained the findings of the special inquest conducted into her death. The jury returned a verdict that the child died from shock due to burns, accidentally sustained whilst playing with a piece of lighted paper and added to their verdict "that a responsible person should be appointed to assist the matron or the assistant matron in their duties especially in regards to the children and that the fireguard

105

should be altered so that the guard should stand further out from the fire and the opening should be kept locked."

The Local Government Board was soon to make contact with the workhouse, and to complain that it had not been informed of the death and that the first they knew about it was when an article in the "Birmingham Daily Post" came to their possession. They demanded the fullest explanation of the incident and also "an explanation from the Medical Officer of his omission to report the occurrence as required by Act 4 of the order of the 4th April 1868."

Dr. Kidd was in trouble for not reporting the incident, but a letter from the Local Government Board was later received dated 9th March 1899 "they will accept the Medical Officer's expression of regret." The Board also promised to check into the way the children were supervised in the workhouse. However, the Guardians seemed to have forgotten their promise and on the 18th April received a reprimand from the Local Government Board - - - "trusting that the subject will receive the serious re-consideration of the Guardians."

CHAPTER SIX

TOWARDS A WELFARE STATE

1. The work of Charles Booth and Seebohm Rowntree.
2. George Lansbury.
3. The 1905 "Royal Commission on the Poor Law and the Relief of Distress".
4. The work of David Lloyd George and his 'People's Budget' of 1909 and the National Insurance Act of 1911.
5. The Depression years and the abolition of the Board of Guardians 1929-1936.
6. The Welfare State begins 1948.

British agriculture faced a depression in the late nineteenth century that lasted until the First World War. A collapse also took place in the steel industry at this time. According to poor relief records, however, the number of registered paupers fell steadily from 1834. In that year 1.25 million paupers were receiving relief (4.3%) and by 1880 the figure had fallen to 808,000 (3%). By 1900 the pauper figure accounted only 2.5%. These figures which seem to illustrate the decline of pauperism are challenged by the findings of two prominent social scientists whose reports in the late 19th century indicate that poverty was still widespread in our major cities, although fewer people were actually claiming official relief. Charles Booth was a wealthy ship-owner and began an investigation into London's poverty extent and structure in the 1880's. His findings filled seventeen volumes and came out from 1889 to 1903 and were called 'Life and Labour of the People in London'. Booth devised a poverty line to aid his results, and this was set at a weekly level of income for a man, wife and three children - it amounted to between 18 shillings and one pound. People who earned less than this figure were regarded as those suffering from poverty. Booth's survey revealed the shocking truth that 35.2% of the population in East London or 30.7% of the population of the city in general lived below the poverty line.   He divided the London poor into four major classes.

Class A.   The lowest class.   This group comprised people such as street sellers, criminals and loafers, and they led a life of extreme hardship.   This class formed 1¼% of the whole population of the city.

Class B.   Casual earners including widows and deserted women and part time labourers.   This group formed 11¼% of the city's population.

Class C.   This groups earnings was regularly hit by trade depressions and form 8% of the total.

Class D.   A group on very low wages of less than 21 shillings a week, and these wages were barely sufficient to keep them alive.   This group formed 14½% of the capital's population.

Benjamin Seebohn Rowntree, son of a wealthy York cocoa manufacturer was intrigued by the work of Booth and wondered whether the London figures applied to all the provincial cities.   He decided to test his theory in his own city of York.   His findings were just as startling as Booth's. He found that 43.4% of the working classes, representing 27.84% of the population of York were living in poverty and some 10% lived in abject poverty in which the total family earnings were well below his poverty line of 21 shillings and 8 pence for a family of husband, wife and three children.   The other 17% lived in secondary poverty in which the total family earnings were barely sufficient for the maintenance of physical efficiency.   His findings were published in 1901 under the title "Poverty: A Study of Town Life".   The findings of both Booth and Rowntree shocked the government by revealing the fact that at least one third of the population suffered the effects of poverty.

Their findings were instrumental in shaming future government into action.   The shadow of the workhouse was slowly to lift over the next thirty years.

The extract below is from Rowntree's book 'Poverty: A Study of Town Life' 1902.

The wage for a labourer in York is from 18s. to 21s.; the minimum expenditure necessary to maintain in a state of physical efficiency a family of two adults and three children is 21s.8d., or, if there are four children, 26s.

The wages paid for unskilled labour in York are insufficient to provide food, shelter and clothing adequate to maintain in a state of bare physical efficiency, even if the diet is less generous than that allowed in the

Workhouse.
And let us clearly understand what 'merely physical efficiency' means. A family living upon the scale allowed for in this estimate must never spend a penny on railway or omnibus; never go into the country unless they walk; never purchase a halfpenny newspaper or buy a ticket for a popular concert; never write letters to absent children, for they cannot afford the postage. They cannot save, join sick club or Trade Union; they cannot pay the subscriptions. The children have no pocket money for dolls, marbles, or sweets. The father must not smoke or drink. The mother must never buy any pretty clothes for herself or her children. 'Nothing must be bought but that which is absolutely necessary for the maintenance of physical health, and what is bought must be of the plainest and most economical description.' Finally, the wage-earner must never be absent from his work for a single day.
If any of these conditions are broken, the extra expenditure is met, and can only be met, by limiting the diet; or in other words by sacrificing physical efficiency.

The growth of the Fabian Society in the 1880's with its belief in socialism also cultivated a new approach to the problem of the poor. The doctrines of 'individualism' and 'self-help' were questioned, and the role of caring governments was discussed. The New Liberalism in the late nineteenth century also affected politicians and thinkers alike, and was to play a more active part in governmental actions in the early twentieth century.

The declining faith in the cult of individualism was strongest amongst a new generation of young thinkers and writers e.g. Beatrice Potter and William Beveridge; who were to make their own contribution to the foundation of the Welfare State in the succeeding years. The advent of the new unions of the unskilled and semiskilled workers focused the attention of government and public on the low paid and poverty. The Matchgirls of Bryant and May's organised a stoppage in 1888. In 1889 the London gas workers took action and this resulted in better working conditions.

Attitudes to poverty and pauperism mellowed due to the increasing voice of the working class in the political arena. The extension of the franchise in 1884 gave thousands more ordinary people a chance to vote and elect governments for the first time. In 1906, as a result of the working class vote, the Parliamentary Labour Party was formed.

Working class figures began to play an important part in the development of social programmes. Will Crooks, was the first person born in a workhouse to become an M.P. George Lansbury was another working class voice in action. The latter, as a result of new Local Government Act of 1894, which allowed women and working men become candidates for election to the Boards of Guardians, became a Guardian in a dockside parish of London. His vivid description of a visit to a workhouse in the early 1890's shows that the dreaded institution had changed little over the sixty years.

"Going down the narrow lane, waiting while an official looked through a grating and hearing his unpleasant voice, made me understand why the poor dreaded these places. I realised how all these prison sort of surroundings were making decent people endure any suffering rather than enter. Officials, whitewashed walls, huge books for name, history, searching, being stripped and bathed in a communal tub, and being dressed in clothes which had been worn by lots of other people - everything possible was done to inflict degradation.

Officers looked upon these people as a nuisance. Clothing was of the usual workhouse type. No undergarments for men or women, boots worn till they fell off. The paupers were allowed out once a month and could be visited once a month. Men were put to stonebreaking or oakum picking. No effort was made to find work for men or women.

On one visit I inspected the supper of oatmeal porridge, with pieces of black stuff floating around. We discovered it to be rat and mice manure. I called for the chief officer, who said the porridge was good and wholesome. 'Very good, madam,' said I, 'here you are, eat one mouthful.' 'Oh dear, no,' said the fine lady, 'the food is not for me, and is good and wholesome enough for those who want it.' I stamped and shouted around till both doctor and master arrived, both of whom pleaded it was all a mistake, and promptly served cocoa and bread and margarine."

The attitude towards the poor and pauperism however continued to improve in the late nineteenth century. A welcome feature was the consideration given to the treatment of elderly paupers, and many of them received specialised and kinder treatment than previously. In 1899 even a pension type or increased allowance on a wholly outdoor relief basis was considered by the government, but nothing came of it.

Unemployment worsened yet again in 1904-5, and resulted in increased relief costs. The government encouraged the founding of 'distress' committees in large urban centres in order to set up schemes to re-deploy the increasing ranks of the unemployed. This move, however, came to nothing due to the orchestrated opposition against it. The increasing agitation over unemployment and poverty in general prompted the government in November 1905 to announce the appointment of a 'Royal Commission on the Poor Law and the Relief of Distress'. This Commission of twenty members was a high powered and well qualified team, and included four top civil servants from the Local Government Board. It included esteemed figures such as Octavia Hill, Charles Booth and Beatrice Webb. It carried out a very detailed enquiry in a much more professional manner than its predecessor of 1832-34 had done, visiting two hundred workhouse Unions, and four hundred workhouses. It also considered the verbal evidence of over four hundred witnesses and over 850 written statements. The commission worked for three years, and their findings filled forty-seven volumes. The main points included a condemnation of the New Poor Law of 1834. It urged more specialization in the treatment of various categories of paupers and criticised the general and mixed type of workhouse. It also demanded that the Boards of Guardians and Poor Law Unions of 1834 should be abolished, and that public assistance authorities should be established in each borough or county. The Commission however was split on a number of deep issues and two main schools of thought prevailed. The supporters of the Minority Report included Beatrice and Sydney Webb and George Lansbury. This group was more radical in its recommendation, and recommended the complete removal of unemployment from local to central government control, under a Ministry of Labour. The group also advocated the setting up of labour exchanges, schemes for re-training, setting up public works.

The second group of Commissioners produced the Majority Report. This report was less radical in its recommmendations. The Minority Report did have an impact in the long term, and certain members of the new Liberal Party of 1903 were influenced by it. The party was determined to wage war on poverty, and soon laid the foundations of the Welfare State; and its Chancellor, David Lloyd George spearheaded the attack on poverty "In so far as poverty is due to circumstances over which man has no control, then the state should step in to the very utmost limit of its resources".

RICH FARE.

' FEE, FI, FO, FAT,
I SMELL THE BLOOD OF A PLUTOCRAT;
BE HE ALIVE OR BE HE DEAD,
I'LL GRIND HIS BONES TO MAKE MY BREAD.'

BERNARD
PARTRIDGE.

*A cartoon depicting David Lloyd George, architect of the
National Insurance, as an ogre.*

The main thrust of the programme took place in 1908 when
state pensions to the over-seventies were provided.   Elderly
people who were British and whose incomes were not above
12 shillings a week, received a pension between 1 shilling
and 5 shillings a week depending on their income.   These
first state pensions were paid at Post Offices, and the trad-
ition continues to this day.   The old and needy were pleased
to receive this regular pension, and this made them less

dependent on the Poor Law, whether for indoor or outdoor relief. As David Lloyd George said "We are lifting the shadow of the workhouse from the homes of the poor". In order to generate the 16 million pounds needed to pay for these pensions and other smaller welfare schemes, the Chancellor was prepared to ride a political storm especially with the House of Lords, and antagonise the wealthy by raising taxation in his 'People's Budget' of 1909 on income, rents, sales of land, tobacco, drink etc. He declared "This is a war budget. It is for raising money to wage implacable warfare on poverty and squalidness".

The climax of social reform in this period was the National Insurance Act of 1911, which came into force in 1913. This tackled some of the problems revealed by Rowntree and Booth and emphasised by the Minority Report. In particular it challenged the poverty caused by illness or temporary unemployment. Point 1 of the Act concerned health insurance. Everyone earning under £160 a year had 1.7p a week deducted from their wages. The employer added 1.25p and the State added a further 0.8p. In return a worker could claim 50p a week sickness benefit for up to 26 weeks and free medical care. Point 2 of the Act covered seven trades where occasional unemployment was a common problem. The worker paid 1p, the employer 1p and the government about 0.7p. The benefit was 35p a week for fifteen weeks, and about 2¼ million workers were covered. This scheme, although rather limited in scope, was a step in the right direction by a caring government, and did much "to remove some of the brambles of poverty". In 1920 the National Insurance Act was extended to cover anyone earning less than £250 a year. The system however was under strain as from the 1929-38 period. The collapse of the American economy in 1929 resulted in disastrous economic and political repercussions in Western Europe. In Britain the old industrial sectors of textiles, coal and shipbuilding collapsed in areas such as the North west, South Wales and North east. Three million workers soon found themselves out of work and this put an enormous burden on the National Insurance system. The initial scheme was based on an expectation of no more than 4% being out of work at any one time. In fact the unemployment rate never fell below 10% for most of the inter-war period. Hundreds of thousands of workers exhausted their fifteen weeks of benefit without any sign of a job, and extended benefits nicknamed the "dole" were introduced as a temporary measure at first. The dole was 'means tested' and caused increased hardships, and even the dole had time limits after which the only thing left was the Poor Law and the workhouse.

The burden on poor relief, increased dramatically, and ratepayers bills in areas worst hit were naturally the highest. The only solution was to shift the financial burden from local ratepayers to the tax payers of the nation, and this was gradually done in stages culminating in the 1934 Unemployment Act (the twenty-first Unemployment Act within the space of fourteen years).

The Unemployment Assistance Board came into operation in 1936, and had offices all over Britain to relieve the overworked Labour Exchanges where benefits were mainly paid. Training centres were also established to teach new skills. Families were encouraged to move from depressed areas or 'special areas' to the Midlands and South-East where the motor car and electrical industries were expanding.

The most profound political decision within this period which affected the 1834 Poor Law Amendment Act was the abolition of the Boards of Guardians of the workhouses. The intent was first published in December 1925, became a Bill in November 1928, and triumphed as an Act in 1929. This therefore was the virtual end of the 1834 legislation. The 625 workhouse Unions from 1929 were inherited by the new County and County Borough Councils, and slowly phased out but never out of mind and memory. Workhouses continued in certain areas until the National Insurance Act of 1946 swept away the system. In 1948 the National Assistance Board was set up which finally put paid to the institution.

IMPORTANT DATES IN THE HISTORY OF THE
BROMSGROVE UNION WORKHOUSE
1834 – 1901

August 1834	The New Poor Law Amendment replaced the Old Poor Law and abolished able-bodied outrelief. Such paupers, henceforth, to be placed in Workhouses.
November 1836	Inaugural meeting in Bromsgrove Town Hall on November 8th to elect Board of Guardians. First meeting of Guardians in the 'old' workhouse on the 21st November.
March 1837	Main officers appointed for the Union. Mr. William Owen and his wife Lucy appointed as the first master and matron.
January 1838	Three pauper boys bound as apprentices to work in Black Country metal-based industries.
February 1838	Thomas Lammas, a troublesome pauper, placed in Droitwich Lunatic Asylum by the Guardians.
August 1838	Attempts by the Guardians at deporting Irish paupers.
November 1838	The Rev. G.R. Gray condemned the Board of Guardians for moving two old women into the workhouse against their will.
February 1839	Miss Owen, aged sixteen years, appointed as the first school teacher of the workhouse children.
March 1839	The new workhouse opened at Gravel Piece Lane.
November 1840 to January 1841	Guardians gave outdoor relief to a few able-bodied paupers.
January 1841	Typhoid fever broke out in Bromsgrove.

January 1842	Death of five year old Henry Cartwright in the workhouse as a result of doctor's negligence.
October 1842	Punishment of Thomas Smith, pauper, began a wave of insubordination amongst the inmates.
November 1842	Epidemic of measles in the workhouse.
January 1843	Typhus fever epidemic in Redditch.
February 1848	A bad month for pauperism. Three hundred and twenty-four inmates in the workhouse.
March 1848	Mutiny of the able-bodied in the workhouse.
November 1848	Action taken against vagrants.
August 1849	Cholera epidemic in the town.
November 1850	Cholera returned to Bromsgrove.
December 1841 to January 1852	Bad attack of smallpox in Bromsgrove.
February 1852	Smallpox epidemic in Redditch.
July 1852	Guardians assisted five local pauper families to emigrate.
January 1859	Dr. Fletcher, M.O.H. for Bromsgrove and Medical Officer of the workhouse condemned the workhouse dietary.
December 1862	Appointment of Mr. and Mrs. Pope as master and matron; this heralded a period of great instability and indiscipline until their dismissal in January 1864.
April 1863	Joseph Webb pauper inmate went berserk in the workhouse.
June 1863	Smallpox ravaged the district.
January 1864	Dismissal of Mr. and Mrs. Pope and the school mistress.
August 1864	Lord Lyttleton of Hagley Hall celebrated sixteen years as Chairman of the Bromsgrove Board of Guardians.
September 1868	Dr. Fletcher further condemned the workhouse dietary.
May 1869	Three pauper boys flogged for absconding from workhouse with workhouse clothing.

116

April 1870	Suicide of Joseph Harris at the workhouse.
June 1871	Pauper boy apprenticed to Samuel Allcock, fishing tackle manufacturer of Redditch.
October 1872	Dr. Fletcher, Medical Officer of the Workhouse, Medical Officer of Health and Public Vaccinator of Bromsgrove District retired after thirty-five years of service to the Union.
September 1873	The Bromsgrove Guardians appealed to the Government against the expansion of state education.
September 1873	The Guardians sanctioned the emigration to Canada of nine small girls from the workhouse.
April 1874	Walter Bladon, Relieving Officer for Redditch in trouble with the Board of Guardians.
August 1877	Typhoid fever broke out in the workhouse.
September 1877	Unfair dismissal of Mr. Allinson, the workhouse master.
January 1878	Bromsgrove Cottage Hospital opened.
December 1878	Dismissal of Mr. and Mrs. Booth as master and matron after just two months of service.
July 1881	Board of Guardians clashed with the Bromsgrove School Board over the question of school fees.
October 1881	Decision of Guardians to close workhouse school room and to send pauper children to Lickey End and Stourbridge Road Board Schools.
November 1881	Measles and scarlet fever attacked Bromsgrove and the workhouse.
September 1882	Suicide of Walter Bladon, Relieving Officer.
October 1885	Headteacher of Lickey End Board School complained to the Guardians of poor attendance of workhouse pupils.
June 1887	Paupers given extra food and allowances

	as part of the celebrations marking Queen Victoria's Jubilee, marking fifty years as monarch.
July 1887	Guardians leased land as a playground for the workhouse children and bought cricket materials.
October 1889	Death of Mr. Wyatt, workhouse master of typhoid fever.
March 1891	Dr. Kidd's confrontation with the Guardians over salary and his dismissal as Medical Officer of Health and Public Vaccinator of Bromsgrove.
January 1892	Mr. H.D. Holloway, Assistant Clerk to the Stourbridge Union, appointed Clerk to the Bromsgrove Union Workhouse.
August 1895	Guardians challenged members of the Bromsgrove U.D.C. to a game of cricket with all 'gate' money to be contributed to poor relief fund.
May 1896	Workhouse boys invited to join the choir of All Saints Church, Bromsgrove.
March 1897	Pauper boy apprenticed to the International Steam Trawling Company of Grimsby.
January 1899	Tragic death of pauper girl, Sarah Ward, aged six, at the workhouse.
February 1901	The end of an era. The death of H.M. Queen Victoria.

BIBLIOGRAPHY

The minute books for the Bromsgrove Board of Guardians for 1836 to 1901. HWRO ref. BA400, Class 251. Parcel Number 1 to 17.

Financial statements for the Unions. HWRO ref BA 2271, class 251.

Orders concerning formation of Poor Law Unions. HWRO ref. BA47, Class 125.1.

Relevant Quarter Sessions material.

'Life and Labour of the People of London' - Charles Booth.

'Poverty: A Study of Town Life' - Benjamin S. Rowntree.

'English Poor Law History' - Webbs.

'The Myth of the Old Poor Law and the Making of the New' by M. Blang.

'The Old Poor Law' 1795-1834 by J.D. Marshall.

'The Relief of Poverty' 1834-1914 by Michael E. Rose.

'Laissez-faire and State Intervention in Nineteenth-Century Britain' by Arthur J. Taylor.

'A Thousand Years of Tardebigge' by M. Dickens.

'The Bygone Bromsgrove Picture Book' by Alan and Sheila Richards.

'My Life' by George Lansbury.

'John Amphlett of Clent' by John Humphreys.

INDEX

120